FAMILY ENRICHMENT WITH FAMILY CLUSTERS

FAMILY ENRICHMENT WITH FAMILY CLUSTERS

MARGARET M. SAWIN

Judson Press® Valley Forge

FAMILY ENRICHMENT WITH FAMILY CLUSTERS

Copyright © 1979
Judson Press, Valley Forge, PA 19481
Second Printing, 1980

Unless otherwise indicated, Bible quotations in this volume are in accordance with the Revised Standard Version of the Bible, copyrighted 1946, 1952, 1971, 1973 © by the Division of Christian Education of the National Council of the Churches of Christ in the United States of America, and used by permission.

Also quoted in this book:

> *The New English Bible*, Copyright © The Delegates of the Oxford University Press and The Syndics of the Cambridge University Press, 1961, 1970.

Library of Congress Cataloging in Publication Data

Sawin, Margaret M.
   Family enrichment with family clusters.

   Bibliography: p.
   Includes index.
   1. Family—United States.   2. Family—
Religious life. I. Title.
HQ535.S26   301.42   78-27253
ISBN 0-8170-0830-6

Dedicated to the memory of

my father
and
my mother

who provided the family unit
in which I had my first learnings
and deepest insights into
productive family living

Preface

A century ago families did not think of themselves as needing to be strengthened; indeed, it was assumed that the family had the necessary strength to help its individual members. Also, the individual family unit could depend on its wider extended family for additional support and concern. A number of other factors reinforced the family in being a strong unit, such as a slowly paced social order, an abundance of natural resources, and the patriotic concept that God favored the nuclear family in the "American way of life." Collectively, these many forces helped to keep the family system intact and strong.

At the conclusion of World War II, a different climate emerged. Technical knowledge and its application escalated. Americans became aware of a larger world outside the United States, while many minority groups came into prominence through the mass media and legal decisions. Turbulence beset the American people during the decade of the sixties. During that period, many persons no longer assumed that the family brought strength and happiness to its members because it was a related unit. Instead, people tested that assumption while pursuing their individual needs and often found the family unit unable to provide that which was taken for granted at one time. As a result, a new concern became needed for appreciation of the family unit and the strengths it brings to its members.

About the same time, new knowledge emerged regarding families as systems while skills were delineated which facilitated interpersonal relationships. These emerged within the thrust which pointed toward self-fulfillment and actualization of one's potential. The family as an actualizing unit without the support from the extended family began to be considered during the seventies. A new kind of support group was needed for the family where it could redeem its strengths and be affirmed.

During the decade of the seventies, new models of religious education were introduced at the same time that churches and church schools suffered a decline. People began to realize that the traditional modes of religious education did not insure Christian living. Since the church is the only institution in our society which has the family within its clientele, it seemed fitting to introduce a mode of religious education for the family within a church context. Moreover, the church's emphasis on valuing and living a fulfilled life befits a process of growth and change for families.

The Family Cluster came into being in 1970; since then it has become the best known form of family enrichment in churches of all faiths and denominations throughout the North American continent. Family enrichment is the process of enriching or deepening the strengths and attributes which a family already possesses in order to provide further growth and fulfillment for its family members, as well as the family unit as a whole. Virginia Satir states that the growth model of learning is based on the notion that people's behavior changes through transactions with other people.[1] The assumption base is that growth and change are positive and energy-producing for further growth. The theological message is that of hope and promise.

The Family Cluster Model is an educational mode of learning for well-functioning families and, therefore, is not therapy nor counseling. These modalities are based on the medical model of pathology and sickness. Enrichment is based on the educational model of normal development and learning.

The Family Cluster's contribution to the wider field of family enrichment is that

- it develops a support group for families in which they can grow and receive caring;
- it enables families to work on their own concerns, questions, hopes, problems, and dreams in order to develop more awareness and self-direction;
- it allows for celebration and worship of the in-depth experiences of life;
- it teaches skills to family members so that they are enabled to live together more harmoniously.

Since there has been no single book written specifically on family enrichment, this book sets forth that modality. Various forms of enrichment which affect the family have been described elsewhere:

- individual enrichment which enhances one individual's growth,
- marriage enrichment which enhances the relationship of the married couple,
- parent enrichment which enhances the relationships between parent and child.

Family enrichment cannot be only for the adults of the family, nor can it be only for one part of the unit. Family enrichment must deal with all members of the family unit as a total human process in itself. The outline of the book includes:

Chapter 1—The family's influence on individuals and need for support groups
Chapter 2—The development of the Family Cluster Model
Chapter 3—How to foster Family Clusters within a congregation
Chapter 4—The various models of family enrichment and a process for selection
Chapter 5—Curriculum and resources for family enrichment
Chapter 6—Leadership within family groups
Chapter 7—Adaptations of the Family Cluster and the need for a total emphasis of family ministries for churches.

This book will be of use to anyone who wants to learn about family enrichment and its implementation in an organized setting.

There are many people to whom I owe appreciation for support and caring during the long emergence of this book. My long-time friends, Rachel and Berner Clarke of Kenmore, New York, shared their love and home during my periods of writing. Liz and Trevor Ewell of Rochester, New York, shared their love and home during the development of the book. Howard Clinebell of Claremont School of Theology gave me the first incentive to attempt writing a book, while Harold Twiss of Judson Press persisted in his attempts to have me write about this concern. My friend Joyce Space typed the manuscript while Tahti Carter served as editor.

I owe an immeasurable degree of gratitude to those families of the First Baptist Church of Rochester, New York, who were willing to risk and experiment with the process of clustering in its beginning years. As a result, they were instrumental in the development of the model. The board of Family Clustering, Inc., provided leadership support and faith in the process, and members still continue to give support and momentum to the model; they are Doris Morgan, Ann Marie Powell, Claude Pullis, Jan Rugh, Lucinda Sangree, and Tom Vander Meulen. Hundreds of individuals and families have provided joy and learnings, as I have conducted workshops and labs in many parts of the North American continent, Australia, and New Zealand. To them I owe appreciation for growing insights into family life and family groups. Both my sister and brother, with their families, have been part of the host of people who provided support and love during times of despair and periods of joy.

"For this reason I bow . . . before the Father, from whom every *family* . . . on earth is named, that according to the *riches* of his glory he may grant you to be *strengthened* with might through his Spirit in the *inner* man" (Ephesians 3:14-16, italics added).

Margaret M. Sawin

Rochester, New York

Contents

CHAPTER 1

The Family: A Forgotten Group

The family is the basic social unit of our human world; it is a microcosm of the larger society. In it we see the fundamental patterns of every human interaction: love and hate, cooperation and competition, trust and rivalry, harmony and conflict, and many others. The family setting provides the training ground for learning to live in the larger world.

In American history, the family had to learn to cope with its physical survival by depending on ingenuity and inner emotional resources. If the extended family lived nearby, it often provided advice, material help, values, support, and moral sustenance. Important in the historical development of the pioneer family was respect for the privacy and autonomy of the family. Removed from the European roots of suppression by royalty, the American family treasured its freedom to be what it wanted to be. Therefore, built into the legal and ethical systems of government was the right for a family unit to have personal independence and privacy.

Changes in Family Life

In the twentieth century the family has changed from a producing institution, where it was primarily self-sufficient, to a consuming institution where it is primarily dependent on many other groups for survival. This dependency has lessened the role of children as workers in the family. With the onset of geographical mobility and increased industrialization, often the nuclear family was removed from its hometown, its extended family, and its ancestral roots. It was forced to rely on its own emotional resources in the new land of suburbia and corporate living. Contrasted to the family of the past, the family of today receives its status and upward mobility from the impersonal corporation or profession. In the case of ethnic families, the history of change is shorter within American society, but the impetus for upward mobility is the same. Families are extraordinarily dependent on "outside" forces and influences, ranging from the nature of the parents' work worlds to the content of TV programming, from the structure of the local school to the organization of health care. Most American families are competing on unequal terms with institutions on which they must depend or which have taken over traditional functions.

The changing role of women is continuing to have a major effect on the family. The woman is no longer confined to the home and child care. She is demanding more equality of opportunity in all fields which have been male-dominated; this has revolutionized the perceptions of male and female roles in every sphere of life. Sexual mores have changed with the inception of "the pill" and the legalization of abortion. A woman is no longer confined to marriage and motherhood unless she so chooses. Long-term commitment to one mate within marriage is rapidly changing.

The mass media has a strategic impact on every home's educational influence and often presents value systems which are different from those of the family or the community. As a result, values and beliefs are influenced significantly without an understanding of the foundations from which they emanate. This makes for rootlessness, constant "searching," and alienation for many persons of all ages. Belief structures are no longer determined by any authoritative fiat.

The family is fragmented time-wise and emotion-wise by its frantic scheduling and involvement in all forms of peer groupings. It seldom has intentional time together and puts little stock in its interpersonal emotional sharing. There are few places in Western society where one can go for emotional sustenance on a day-to-day basis, since many of society's groups are based on competition, suspicion, and accomplishment. Success is measured by one's ability to achieve a higher standard of living, based on the accumulation of goods. As a result, striving and straining become substitutes for the family values of generosity, frankness, and love. Douglas Anderson states that the effect this has upon family intimacy is dichotomous; these family values become crucial to maintain yet more difficult to achieve.[1]

The more impersonal and confusing our society becomes, the more desperately its members need primary relationships through which they can develop their process of identity and achieve a sense of worth. They need a primary group in which to experience the warmth of love and acceptance; they need a close-knit group in which to find healing and renewal from life's crises. The family is the prime group in which children experience this, while often it is the only group in which adults may share in such intimacy. Philippe Aries, the European historian of the family, says, "The family has come to be both an all-purpose refuge and a prison [of love]."[2] In its isolation, the nuclear family must provide those attributes which the wider extended family once supplied; at the same time the limitation of close relations for the family serves to confine and to restrict. With the increase in the number of one-parent families, the one adult must sustain himself or herself as well as the younger members of the family; this becomes a heavy burden and a difficult task. Clearly, the family unit within isolation cannot fulfill all its responsibilities and still be the sustaining reference for all its family members. The family unit needs to be supported and nourished.

The Need for Care of the Family Unit

It has long been known that the family has the strongest, most intense effect on individuals in their development; but the concept of the family, as a system in need of care and nurture, is a new notion in our society. If we expect individuals within the family to give and to receive love and acceptance, we must see that the family, as a complete unit, receives warmth and support. Formerly, this help was provided by nearby extended family members or persons within close-knit neighborhoods. With mobile suburban populations and changing apartment dwellers, the supports which once came to the aid of a family are no longer there. Churches used to provide support and care; but many now stress numerical growth and organization, neglecting small, caring groups within their structures. No agency in our country has considered ongoing support of the family as its major task.

Our society has tried to amend this by providing support structures with individual family members in public schools, social work agencies, and mental health units; but often these agencies offer their aid only after a family has become dysfunctional and is in difficulty. We have not reached the point of realization that such structures cannot change individuals while neglecting the family system in which that individual lives. The family is the great burden carrier of the social order, bombarded on all sides by the institutions, the laws, and the popular cultures of the society. In comparison with other agencies, it is organizationally inferior. It is heavily weighted with dependents who are limited in age and experience, and it does not have the freedom as do other institutions to reject its weak members in order to recruit more competent teammates. Moreover, no one teaches family members the skills by which the family can function more smoothly. One of the cultural shibboleths is that a family loves you no matter what you do! However, there is little help for the family in dealing with a "weak" or "incompetent" member who affects the family in a destructive manner.

Support Groups for the Total Family

A growing number of persons are aware of the need to provide support groups for the total family unit so that it can be connected with other families in ways modern living does not permit naturally. Since the extended family, related by blood or marriage, has diminished, we need to create new kinds of family groups for support and affection. Richard Farson, of the Family Service of America, has said that a network of families would not only support each other in times of crisis but also "monitor each other's family lives."[3] This opportunity would provide feedback to the family as to how it is operating in light of the goals it has set for itself. Such support and concern can become a model of the New Testament *koinonia* or a caring fellowship of the people of God. A support group would enable children to belong to a behavioral community from which they learn fellowship. It would enable adolescents to share in the caring process and thus feel a sense of belonging. It would enable adults to be relieved of the sole responsibility for the emotional sustenance of the family system and even more so at times of crisis. For the complete system of the family, it would enable the family to realize that it is important to others, that it is worthy of affirmation, and that it can depend on others for support and affection.

What could happen in support groups of families? There are many complex interactions and opportunities for growth changes. Douglas Anderson has termed this kind of group a "Family Growth Group." After interviewing leaders of such groups, he developed a list of features which characterize Family Growth Groups:

"1. The participation of the whole family as a unit
2. The strengthening of families and the release of their potential for growth at the normal crises of the family life cycle

3. The realization of family potential in 'peak moments' of joy and deep sharing within families
4. In-depth sharing between families
5. A sense of 'connectedness' and community through involvement with people outside the family
6. Enabling families to care for and help one another, including the exchange of mundane services
7. Helping families to 'invent their own futures,' setting and achieving their own goals while using feedback from members of other families as 'consultants'
8. Use of simulations, games and media technology to introduce novel environmental input into families and to enable them to learn new modes of problem-solving and conflict resolution
9. Exposure of other families, leading to openness to the points of view of others and to involvement in the wider community
10. Intergenerational activity and conversation that 'enables' different generations to become a significant part of each other's lives
11. Interfamily influencing of values and attitudes and the exploring of new value systems
12. Interfamily help in child rearing, expecially through the provision of alternative adult role models
13. Respect and valuing of privacy, without it becoming 'privatism'
14. Fun with family recreation and entertainment."[4]

It is apparent that many of the characteristics the extended family once shared can be utilized in this new type of grouping, thereby providing a sense of bondedness and connectedness with other families. At the same time, there is an emphasis on growth and change which is needed in a "future shock" society. Many of the so-called ills of the family are due to neglect in the area of prevention. There is seldom any kind of intervention in the typical family as problems develop into crises. Family members "stumble through," without knowledge of skills or outside help, until the situation explodes into crisis proportions, with resulting devastation. A family growth group also can provide a sense of joy and hope for families as they share their successes and dreams; this enables change to be approached with anticipation and celebration as part of God's plan for life in the twentieth century. In many respects a family growth group is a larger "faith family" in pilgrimage.

Learning Within the Family Setting

Our culture is conditioned by schools and other educational institutions to think that learning takes place only within the formal structure of education. Very little has been written on how the family unit itself is an educator of great intensity and excessive strength. Hope Jensen Leichter sums up this influence by stating that "the family is an arena in which virtually the entire range of human experiences can take place." These cover every emotion, every type of behavior, and every subject of content area. Moreover, the family may provide "conscious, systematic instruction to repetitive moment-to-moment influences."[5] Not only do children learn from parents, but also parents learn from children; children learn from each other, as well as parents from each other in an ongoing process. Learning within the family is a cyclical, ongoing process which has repercussions throughout a person's life.

At the same time the child is developing in the family, the adult/parent is working through new relationships of parenthood which are modeled often after the adult's former child/parent relationships. Also, adults move through their own developmental "passages" which appear to occur every seven or eight years. The parents, as a married couple, move through their stages of relational "we-ness." Therefore, a family consists of a number of persons in their individual stages of growth as well as subgroup stages of growth in the family's development. Each stage brings change. When these kinds of changes within families are coupled with society's changes, there results a greater need for coping than we have ever known before. No wonder family life is so complicated!

When members of a family are engaged in a learning process together within a family growth group, there are dynamic factors operating in the total family unit which enable the individual to internalize quickly new learnings within the family system. Children observe their parents' struggle with their own interaction process. They become aware of the difficulties involved in changing learning patterns and beliefs. At the same time, children and youth observe other parents' work on similar tasks, noting differences between adults' styles of functioning. Adults observe their children in the learning process, as well as other children and youth. Children become models for adults within a legitimate learning setting, as there is the emergence of differing life-styles, value systems, and roles. In a period of social revolution, people need access to differing options for discovering alternatives from which to choose. As change becomes a constant in life, generations need each other to explore new patterns of living. Margaret Mead has commented that "all of us who grew up before World War II are . . . immigrants . . . in a new age."[6] Conditions are different in a highly technical, industrialized society, and our own growing-up process did not prepare us to live in such an era. This promotes guilt and anxiety when we, as adults, do not know about a world in which we are responsible for the upbringing of children.

In a family grouping, families can observe other complete family units in various experiences of communication, decision making, conflict resolution, etc. This provides modeling for some of the crucial elements of living today within a family. Family members can observe the relationships of others in comparison with their own. They can decide intentionally if they want to keep the behaviors resulting from past family influences or if they want to change some behaviors. Some children and youth will recognize that the behaviors of their family lives are productive and fulfilling, thus enabling them to be more satisfied with the way their family operates. With the presence of the complete family, all are involved in the learning together; difficulties are avoided which occur when one person returns to the family with new ideas and behaviors and tries to get the others to change.

In today's pluralistic world, families are thrust into so much change that they are not aware of the needs for learning specific skills to cope with these alternatives. The adults did not experience such education within their "families of origin"; so they have no models from which to learn. We are bombarded with choices and alternatives from which intentionalized decisions need to be made. Clare Buckland has listed the kinds of competencies deemed important for a family system to operate constructively in the "post-industrial society"[7]:

> clarification of values;
> self-determination of family patterns;
> parental modeling of desired behaviors;
> acceptance of differences;
> economy in decision-making, assent and commitment;
> balance between authority, control and autonomy;
> minimal discontinuity between the worlds of adult and child, home and
>   community;
> expansion of the child's role.[8]

Most families have not delineated such a list nor developed skills to meet these needed competencies for society living in which we are already engaged. Buckland suggests that when all the family members participate together, behavioral change is accelerated in the intended direction.[9] This is especially true when families participate in a family growth group together; the process of learning is hastened. Families, as systems, are taught in a way so they are not caught in their usual "loggerheads" which hinder learning and change. Family education cannot be education for the adults only nor education for the children only; family education must deal with all members of the family together as a total human process in itself.

What Is a Healthy Family?

Family growth groups are educational in nature and not treatment oriented. They deal with healthy families who want to learn to function in more wholesome ways. It is difficult to find adequate language to describe a family which is functioning productively. Studies of the family and subsequent writings reflect this ambiguity. If we say a family is healthy, the implication is that the opposite is unhealthy or sick; yet many families are in between—they are not completely healthy in their functioning nor completely broken down in their dysfunctioning. Many are void of emotional closeness and are described as "empty shell families" by William Goode, family sociologist.[10] Most studies of families in our society have been conducted within the context of the medical model—or the environment of pathology. Someone or some system is described as sick and as needing a doctor, a psychiatrist, or a counselor to diagnose and facilitate the healing process. The inference is that a dysfunctional person or family needs expert help to get well. This concern has been addressed by Herbert Otto who suggests that our culture is "pathology-oriented" with the bias that the study of illness and dysfunction is the route for understanding health and optimal functioning.[11]

Contrasted to the medical model is the "growth" or "potential" model. This model assumes that the system or members of the system are well and functioning, but that they can keep growing by learning ways to enhance further their relationships. This growth brings more fulfillment to the members in relationship, thus helping the family system to have deeper meaning. The educational model suggests that individuals want to learn to behave in different ways without the need to justify the teaching that a "client" or "student" or "learner" is moving from "sick" (or maladaptive, maladjustive) behavior to "well" (or adjusted, adaptive) behavior. A growth program may be established on the basis that the individual—or the human system—wants to learn some different behaviors. This takes the stigma off the "patient" (or "client") as one who *needs* something and emphasizes the "student" (or "pupil") as one who *wants* to learn something. Those who advocate growth and enrichment do so not only for the sake of preventing dysfunctioning but also for the sake of fulfilling or actualizing what is potentially present but may not be used to its fullest. Herbert Otto, who has conducted research on family strengths, states:

> It is crystal clear that families function at a very small fraction of their potential and that the possibilities and potentialities of family living remain largely to be explored.[12]

There has been much idealization about the family, but little research has been conducted on what characteristics are those of a functioning family. A recent addition to the literature is the book *No Single Thread*, written by a psychiatric team in Dallas, Texas. The book was stimulated by the interest of a Methodist minister who suggested the team needed to know the "healthy direction" toward which they were pointing dysfunctional families within their clinical practice.

Basically, the team found there was "no single thread," or one characteristic, which helped a family to function optimally. Some of the eight identified characteristics of such families were:

1. Their encounters with each other and with those persons outside the family were generally caring and empathetic.
2. There was respect for differences in belief, and freedom of expression in statements of agreement or disagreement. No one person told the other family members what to believe, but there was a strong core around a few basic beliefs.
3. When approaching problems, numerous options were encouraged and explored. No single approach nor absolute authority was utilized in problem solving.
4. The parental marriage bond was effective in meeting the needs of both parents, so they could relate to each other effectively and model this means of relating to the children. The children learned about effective conjugal relationships from this example.
5. The children expressed opinions which were considered and negotiated, but the power was clear within the family structure.
6. These families encouraged personal autonomy where each

individual could be his or her own person. As a result, they communicated clearly, and each person was respected and acknowledged by the others. There was strong emphasis for each individual to accept responsibility for his or her own feelings, thoughts, and actions. Conflict was faced openly and of short duration because of the ability to resolve it to the satisfaction of family members.[13]

A strong, functioning family has an open, flexible system of organization; so it is not rigid nor closed to outside changes or individual desires. This means roles are flexible; rules are appropriate and subject to change. Some persons call these "growth-oriented families."[14] Satir writes of such a family in this way:

> I feel that if I lived in such a family, I would be listened to and would be interested in listening to others; . . . I would feel like a person in my own right—noticed, valued, loved, and clearly asked to notice, value, and love others. . . . People look *at* one another, not *through* one another or at the floor; and they speak in rich, clear voices. . . . The children . . . seem open and friendly, and the rest of the family treats them very much as persons.
>
> People seem comfortable about touching one another and showing their affection, regardless of age. The evidence of loving and caring [is shown] . . . by talking openly and listening with concern, by being straight and real with one another. . . .
>
> Members of a nurturing family feel free to tell each other how they feel. *Anything* can be talked about— the disappointments, fears, hurts, angers, criticisms as well as the joys and achievements.[15]

The Role of the Church in Stimulating Family Growth Groups

Traditionally the church has been an institution which has claimed growth and change to be essential parts of the Christian faith for individuals. However, it has not been always an institution which practices change. Increasingly we have become aware of the influence of the family system on individuals, and the church could become the institution which would facilitate growth and affirmation for the human system of the family. However, this calls for a change from the traditional Sunday school programming by peer groups which separates family members. A ministry to total families would be a new mission for the church.

The church is the only agency in Western civilization which has all the members of the family as part of its clientele. It is the only organized group which reaches persons through the complete life cycle from birth to death. Its scriptural heritage provides a motive for exploring values and beliefs with a process, open-ended approach.

Many parents and adults do not have a clear idea of what is to be taught in belief areas incorporating values, truths, and morals because they themselves do not have a clear conviction of their own beliefs. They were often raised in a simplistic belief persuasion which no longer is adequate for a complicated, changing world. They may know what beliefs they have shed but often do not possess amended religious patterns which could provide newer forms of security and direction. There has been a loss of authority from which values and morals were once pronounced in the society, which has been described by Margaret Mead as "a crisis in faith." Persons have lost not only their faith in religion but also in political ideology, science, and the "expert." ". . . they have been deprived of every kind of security." [16]

With this type of faith crisis, parents are unable to share a security of belief patterns with children; often their behavioral modeling is inconsistent with their outmoded shibboleths. Children will inevitably follow the behavioral actions over parental words. Many parents are "too uncertain to assert old dogmatisms" [17] but do not possess renewed belief patterns which could affirm their present convictions. The church could meet a tremendous need by encouraging discussions of values and beliefs within the intergenerational context of the family. There is a "strong ideological hunger which would give coherence to a person's world, yet the acceptable factors are often of a fragmentary nature. [18]

The family setting is that in which an individual first experiences and learns the meaning of "bondedness," "belongingness," and "connectedness" which build healthy interpersonal relations. This is the beginning of faith and security which can later be developed into a trust relationship with a Higher Being—God. Therefore, religious nurturance and education must begin with the adults within the home. As they wrestle with faith issues, make value decisions, and commit themselves to a life-style congruent with these, children develop faith and trust from the modeling of those significant adults. In a family approach to religious education, a model of New Testament belief is established which children observe and learn as the behavior of Christians. Adolescents are a normal part of the caring process as they participate in the behaviors of "bondedness" and group responsibility. The adults are able to explore needed areas of change within a trust climate of freedom. The family, as a whole, can make choices and begin to intentionalize behaviors congruent with those choices. This results in productive, functional relating within the everyday life of the family where the basic faith issues are explored and lived. As a result, a family becomes more actualized, more healthy, more productive. This, in turn, has an influence in all sectors of society where that family interacts: school, work, church, neighborhood, community. This "abundant living" is the core meaning of the New Testament. To affirm and celebrate a complete family, amidst its strivings, joys, concerns, sorrows, is almost unheard of! We simply do not have the institutional modes which deal with the family as a unit. This can be the mission of the twentieth-century Christian church—to influence its families, as human systems, for living and growing abundantly in a world of "future shock."

The following chapters present the manner in which family enrichment can be initiated in local congregations. Included are descriptions of various models of family enrichment, particularly the Family Cluster Model. Resources, curriculum planning, leadership and other factors important to successful use of family models are in the various chapters. Family enrichment is utilized by congregations of all denominations and faith groups, so it is an advocacy which can be undertaken by any institution which believes in the cause of abundant living within the family.

CHAPTER 2

The Development of the
Family Cluster Model

My personal involvement in family growth groups emanated from my doctoral research in human development and learning. As a religious educator for twenty years, I had been involved professionally in the furtherance of the traditional modes of the profession; so it was natural to conduct a study on Sunday church school teachers for my doctoral project. I chose to consider the personality characteristics of 259 Protestant female Sunday church school teachers of children within forty-three churches of four major denominations in greater Washington, D.C. Then I correlated those characteristics with the perceptions the Sunday school teachers had in regard to the behavior of children in general. It was my conviction that a communicator of the Christian faith—which is how I perceived Sunday church school teachers—must be congruent in words and actions; therefore, habitual traits of personality are important in assessing the impact of the teacher as a person. To assess personality characteristics, the Edwards Personal Preference Schedule[1] was utilized because of its extensive use in studies conducted among church populations. When the results were collated, two variables of personality were revealed among the church school teachers which did not appear to be congruent with characteristics of persons professing the Christian faith. These characteristics were known as nurturance and succorance[2], according to Edwards. Compared with a large number of the female population in the United States, the teachers were *less* willing to receive support and caring from others. These communicators of the Christian faith neither wished to be involved wholeheartedly in the nurturance of others nor wanted to have other persons help and share affection with them. If the Christian community of the church school is to be one of comfort, assistance, and promotion of interpersonal growth, these teachers were behaving in the opposite direction from the scriptural traits of the Christian community.[3] In reviewing other studies conducted with church school teachers, it appeared that many do not possess the personality characteristics which would enable them to model the manner of living expected in a faith community.[4] If the content (taken from the Scriptures) a teacher talks about in the classroom is incongruent with how she behaves, the results may be evidenced in confusion, lack of belief, and insecurity about the meaning of the gospel. Don Hamachek suggests that a teacher is a model for appropriate behavior and "that students . . . assume, and ultimately reflect (probably unconsciously) those personal characteristics most dominant in the teacher."[5]

From reflection on these studies, I became aware that Christian education needed some models different from the classroom model of the Sunday church school. In my developmental studies of the manner in which humans evolve in a faith process, I became aware that the family has a profound influence on the nurturance of a religious belief system; yet the church does very little to help families and parents in their task of nurturing. Also, I realized that the time, energy, and budget spent in keeping large church buildings in operation needed to be reversed. A prime educational task of the church is to facilitate parents in fulfilling their roles as religious nurturers within the family. Religious *education* is formalized teaching about a specific religious belief structure. Religious *nurturing* is learning from the combination of informal life experiences and word meanings which interpret such experiences. Religious education cannot be taught effectively without a foundation of religious nurturing. Harry Emerson Fosdick has been credited with saying, "Christian education is learning about that which you've already caught." We "catch" nurturant patterns and belief behaviors from others through the process called "modeling," and modeling is most apt to occur between persons who are relationally significant. Most church school teachers are not significant persons in children's lives today; moreover, the research shows that often they do not model scriptural truths. In fact, they may be teaching the opposite!

In the spring of 1969, I corresponded with a number of family sociologists, religious educators, and developmental psychologists to discuss where family groups might be meeting in educational settings. The replies were strikingly similar: the "experts" said the idea was a good one, but they knew of no one doing it. From that time I acquired a new vision: that of developing family education in the church to facilitate interpersonal religious growth of members within the family unit. My pilgrimage continued through becoming Minister of Education at the First Baptist Church of Rochester, New York, in 1969.

Developing the Model

In 1970, I experimented with a model[6] of family education—or family enrichment—which I chose to name the "Family Cluster." The definition of a Family Cluster has evolved as the model has emerged; we now know the realities important to the meaning of a Family Cluster.

A Family Cluster is a group of four or five complete family units* which contract to meet together periodically over an extended period of time for shared educational experiences related to their living in relationship within their families. A Cluster provides mutual support, training in skills which facilitate the family living in relationship, and celebration of their life and beliefs together.

(*A family unit is made up of any persons who live in relationship with one another, i.e., a nuclear family, a one-parent family, a couple without children, one or more persons who live in one household, a single person who lives alone but has relationships with others.)

With the support of the board of Christian education of the church, we started Family Clusters with two pilot experiments ten weeks in length. During this time, also, I maintained a full program of Christian education throughout the church, as well as developing some other innovative models. The two clusters emerged from nine families who were interested in enriching their lives, some of whom were discouraged with the church school approach to Christian education. With this motivation, I felt it was necessary to discover what these families might expect to happen in a cluster, as well as to share what experiences might be possible in an intergenerational grouping of families. I decided to call on families in their homes for their final commitment; thus began the concept of family contracting which will be described in a later chapter. Someone suggested that the supper hour would be a good time during which to meet; so it was decided that each family would bring its own sandwiches for a shared meal. It became evident that eating together was a significant part of building relations. Our two pilot clusters contained these dimensions: Cluster A contained four nuclear families: ten children, ages three to twelve; eight adults, plus one leader; Cluster B included five nuclear families: twelve children, ages five to fourteen; and ten adults, plus one leader.

We began with get-acquainted exercises for individuals and then for families as units. Our second session saw the development of a group contract regarding meal preparations, cleanup, the care of younger children, freedom to participate or not participate in particular exercises, and the handling of absences. By the third session, we began communication exercises such as:

- having family members draw pictures of self-perception and other-perception in their families (perceptual uniqueness and self-concept);
- having families build Tinker-Toy models from instructions individual members repeated to the rest of the family (increasing levels of feedback);
- having persons respond to pictures and quotes on communication (introducing ideas and knowledge);
- playing the "Broken Squares" game[7] (nonverbal effectiveness in completion of a task);
- having persons in "pretend" or "simulated" families discuss communication problems (interfamily sharing and learning);
- using the story of Suzuki Beane,[8] read serially (illustration of differences in life-styles of families).

By the sixth session it became clear that families were beginning to be aware which of their communication patterns were helpful and which were not helpful to growth. The "uncomfortable" phase of group relations was beginning to develop; persons were aware of differences and problems among families and unsure about how to deal with them in the group. A few adults talked with me in private about it. It was an uneasy time for the group process, but somehow we weathered the storm! Children became aware of their part in the cluster and began to remind parents what the agreement (contract) included for membership in the Family Cluster. About this time evaluation was incorporated also, with opportunity for persons to tell what they liked and what they wished would be different. The children had asked for some group recreation time; so we incorporated a game/fun period. A new topic on "poverty" was chosen by consensus, and the clusters were into their second state of development by about the seventh session. I was leader of both clusters—both studying the same themes—but it became evident that they were following different patterns because of the uniqueness of the individuals and families in each. What worked in one group was not necessarily appropriate for the other! At the conclusion of the contracted period (ten sessions, one per week of two hours in length), we had a party to celebrate our being together. A number of children and adults asked if they could have more cluster sessions, and six of the nine families requested the board of Christian education to continue a family-type religious educational experience in the fall calendar. A few persons did not find the experience to be "religious" in nature, according to their perceptions. This resulted in many discussions of what religious education is and how it is defined in program!

Ann Marie Powell, a family member and church volunteer, asked to become a cluster leader for the fall; so we found some opportunities for her to take leadership training related to skills in cluster leadership. In September the six families became nuclei for the formation of three clusters, with Ann Marie leading one and I the other two. Other families were recruited by contracting, and the board of Christian education accepted this as an alternative form of Christian education. Most cluster families still attended the traditional segments of the church's educational programs. Family Clusters had moved beyond the beginning stages and were becoming part of the educational program.

In January, 1971, three graduate students from the Department of Pastoral Counseling at the Divinity School of Colgate-Rochester/Bexley Hall/Crozer joined Ann Marie Powell and me in coleading the three clusters. They received credit toward a course in family systems. An introductory training program for leaders was introduced by Dr. Edward Thornton, pastoral psychologist, who also served as our consultant.

In the fall of 1971, two other churches in Rochester started family clusters, and we were faced with the process of training leaders for family groups. This resulted in an ongoing, in-service leadership program, as it became evident that most clusters needed two leaders per group. Leadership development became a way to refine the model. Further developments in leadership training evolved, and they are described in a later chapter.

Goals and Theoretical Foundations of the Model

During these periods of clustering within several churches, basic goals began to emerge out of the empirical observations of the leaders. These were refined and used to provide an evaluative framework for the next grouping of clusters. These goals also gave the model a sense of direction and clarity when we were sharing it with others. Realization of the complex variables, out of which clusters operate, came into view as several persons utilized the model in different sections of the country. There were also numerous observers from different disciplines, as well as family members from various vocations, who contributed background thinking to the development of the model.

A basic premise of the Family Cluster Model is that the *system of the family* provides the most intensive framework for growth and change. Each family system is affirmed for what it is, each is encouraged to change and grow, and each is supported in the new behaviors it tries. The basic goals of the Family Cluster Model are:

1. To provide an intergenerational group of family units where children can relate easily to adults and adults to children;
2. To provide a group which can grow in support and mutuality for its members;
3. To provide a group where parents can gain perspective about their own children through contact with other children and other adults' perceptions of their children; likewise, where children can gain perspective about their own parents through contact with other parents and other children's perceptions of their parents;
4. To provide an opportunity for families to consider experiences seriously related to themselves as individuals, as family members, as group members, and as members of a faith community;
5. To provide a group wherein there is opportunity for families to model for each other aspects of their family systems in communication, decision making, disciplining, interrelating, problem solving, etc.;
6. To provide a joint experience between generations where adults can share their concerns regarding the meaning of life's experiences for them amidst a time of rapid social changes and aberration of traditional values; children can deal existentially with their real world experiences, using the group as a place to check out their experiences amidst its support and value system;

7. To help families discover and develop their strengths through increased loving, caring, joy, and creating;
8. To provide an opportunity for positive intervention into family systems so as to facilitate their living and growing together more productively.

In an empirical model, a person begins experimenting from certain value assumptions, and the model takes shape from the various phenomena which develop. Variables or parts are assigned names, with certain meanings given to those terms. The same was true of the Family Cluster Model. It started with some basic assumptions which grew out of studies and research related to human beings and family systems. Each individual is unique and, therefore, perceives her or his experiences differently from everyone else. With the uniqueness of each individual, a family unit is unique as it begins with two adults who care for each other. Children born to those adults bring another interaction dimension of uniqueness to the family. The family provides the greatest influence on children, as well as supplying an impact on the potentialities of the adults. The growth or human potential perspectives consider individuals and families to be in an evolving process which moves toward more fulfillment or actualization. Learning is accomplished through a myriad of experiences and interactions, and the learning of religious behaviors can be greatly affected by interaction with "significant other persons" within small groups.

It became clear that there were several theoretical foundations of knowledge which contributed to understanding the Model's complexity; as various people utilized the Model, these understandings were confirmed. There are five synthesizing concepts from basic disciplines of theory and research which provide a fundamental foundation to the Family Cluster Model. First, the basic premise is that the *system of the family* provides the most forceful structure for growth and change. Each family is an interwoven group of human components related in a cause and effect manner; these individuals provide reciprocal relationships to each other and to the family as a group. These relationships become stabilized over time so that they are predictable and observable. Each individual in the family influences others through a myriad of verbal and nonverbal clues; if we want to affect the behaviors and learnings of one person in the family, we must reach the whole system. By exposing all family members together in a learning situation, each is subjected and influenced in his own perceptive fashion by the others and by the unit as a whole. There are usually four or five family systems in each cluster, making an approximate total of twenty-five to thirty individuals, depending on the number of people in each system. The knowledge for family systems comes from family therapy, multi-family therapy, and family sociology.

The four or five family systems meet together in a *group*, known as a Family Cluster; so a second area of knowledge is group dynamics. Each developing group has certain dynamics at work between its members and among its subsystems of families, which make the "ground rules" considerably different from those in a group made up of individual peers. In this capacity, the Family Cluster presents a uniqueness to the group work movement. A group provides a powerful environment for change, and the cluster group is facilitated to become supportive for both individuals and families in order to build trust; this in turn enables risk taking and change. There is *intra*-family exchange as well as *inter*-family exchange, which helps the cluster group to become often like an extended family. The manner in which leadership is exerted is a powerful force in group modeling, and various kinds of leadership behavior are used by the group facilitators. Knowledge of group dynamics and leadership drawn from the field of social psychology provide information for this area.

Third, a Family Cluster is a *growth* model—or a *change* model—which facilitates movements toward the actualizing of a family's strengths and potential. The knowledge for this foundational theory comes from humanistic psychology which centers on the uniqueness of human persons and their inner desire to grow toward more fulfillment of their potential; the same can be true of individuals as they make up the family system. In this format, the individual can influence the system; the system can influence the individual, while the cluster group provides support and momentum. Families are encouraged to discover their latent resources and to experiment with them in new behaviors. This offers the family system more options and choices in a fast-changing world. The family becomes aware of its ability to move in directions of importance to family members; thereby it becomes more actualized and fulfilled. They are encouraged to build on their strengths and joys as well as their dreams and hopes. This approach empowers individuals so they are able to cope more effectively with problems and crises. Humanistic psychology, as well as transpersonal psychology, contribute knowledge in this area.

In the fourth place, the process in the cluster which promotes growth is that of *experiential education,* whereby reflected experiences rather than didactic content become the core of the learning activity. Educating experientially is particularly relevant to faith learning, as well as applicable to all age groups. Since all the members of a cluster have been or are in some kind of family system, a common family "exercise" is used which involves active participation. From this experience individuals can reflect on their feelings and learnings. In this action/reflection manner, persons can move into analyzing and discussing the ways they hope to transfer these new learnings to their family system at home. With all the family members present, the opportunity for "back-home realization" is greater. The curriculum or content of a cluster is garnered from the concerns, questions, problems, hopes of the families in the group; this makes a more difficult model for which to plan than models which have a set curriculum of content or skills. The knowledge for this foundation area is contributed by learning theory and educational psychology.

Finally, a cluster experience is based on *process theology,* whereby the belief process is facilitated from persons' individual experiences, which are valid and authentic for each person. All of life's experiences can have religious interpretations. The area of transpersonal theology suggests there is a transcendent power known as God/Spirit/Force/Energy which substantiates each person's existence. This Spirit is always present to individuals and accessible through prayer, meditation, contemplation, Bible study, reading, interrelating, etc. The process of believing, sharing the meanings of that belief through both words and behavior, and receiving feedback on behavior are ways to further growth in faith. Each individual is on her or his own faith pilgrimage and can share that journey with others; persons absorb and internalize the values of others who help them most to meet their needs. In this process, a person is constantly fashioning her or his own value/belief system from which evolves a behavioral stance. This gradually becomes a life-style. Since the emotional and cognitive factors of a person's belief system are first formulated within family interactions, it is necessary to work with families for education in a faith system. The basic elements of belief—trust, autonomy, initiative, integrity—are built out of the psychodynamics of interpersonal relationships which have their greatest impact from the family. These five dynamics—family systems, group process, growth forces, experiential education, and process theology—become synthesized in a cluster and provide momentum for family change. In turn, this affects each individual within the most powerful human system.

Uniqueness and Adaptability of the Model

Since the family is part of every type of population, Family Clusters have been used in many groups among numerous denominations and faiths. It has been tried in Jewish synagogues, on military bases, with clergy families, families of seminarians, and in some ethnic groups. The model lends itself to ready adaptation. As the families in a cluster determine what it is they want and need to work on, skilled leaders need to plan with the families around their own agendae. The model has been used mostly with middle-class, white families, although several clusters have had mixtures of families of differing socioeconomic levels as they reflect the congregation or organization at large. It has been tried in two neighborhood public schools with black families, and another pilot took place with families from an integrated public school.

In our culture, where the single person is omitted from many of the social functions, the Family Cluster can readily incorporate such a person into its membership. A single person contracts to be in the cluster as does any other type of family. He or she becomes an ongoing part of the cluster activities and agreement. Planning or designing for a cluster with single persons needs to be done with this variable in mind. Simulated families and other kinds of groupings make it feasible to include the single person easily into activities. Many times adolescents want to know what the life-style of a single person is like, and such may be shared with them as well as with other persons. With the inclusion of singles, the outstanding feature of the cluster is to provide a covenant group in which an individual can experience belongingness and acceptance. At the same time, a single person of any age can make a powerful contribution to the group, thereby acknowledging the gifts of each individual toward the building of community.

The Family Cluster provides a number of unique experiences which few other educational programs offer. It works on an emerging design process, which means that each group of families works on what is important to them. This is experiential theology at its best!

All persons in the cluster are exposed to growth processes, so it readily becomes a learning experience for everyone; there are not "little" people and "big" people in cluster—there are only people with different types and years of experiences. The process of modeling works in every direction: adults model from children; children model from older children and adolescents, as well as adults; families model from other families; all persons model various forms of relationships. The presence of God is affirmed as it flows from each person to every other one.

The family system, in which primary concepts of self and others are learned, is opened to change and development, so the system facilitates individual growth. Interactions become more reciprocal. Interrelationships of nurture and growth within the primary system are highlighted and affirmed. These can be utilized within the everyday living of the family within the home. Family Clusters often become groups of mutual support and sharing so that they become "the church" in actuality for their members as the Clusters foster the sense of God's presence in relationships.

The Family Cluster appears to be an easy model to implement; however, the concept of grouping family systems in a growth model introduces a number of variables unknown in any other kind of grouping. Most public school and church education systems are built on peer groupings with a teacher/curriculum mode of educating. The Family Cluster is built on family systems with a facilitator/need-based mode of educating. There are great differences between the two modes, and it behooves a leader to understand these. Some of the dynamics operant are:

- a number of individuals of all ages,
- families at all stages of growth,
- the cluster group at its stage of development in the growth process,
- the two leaders and their relationships with each other, with the group, with individuals or subgroupings within the cluster,
- subgroupings of males, females, or peers,
- subgroupings of couples in relationship,
- intergenerational subgroupings,
- siblings of various ages,
- parent/child relationships at various stages, manifesting diverse kinds of behavior,
- the expectations of a sponsoring organization.

Amidst all these complexities, families and individuals do change! The following quote is a testimony from a family which has been in the growth process for six years as individuals, a married couple, and a family unit within a cluster:

The "change" you started in our lives (six years ago) by asking "why" and showing "how" is continuing. Our living is exciting, more fulfilling, and searching for that which is most meaningful to us.

CHAPTER 3

Fostering Family Clusters
in a Church Setting

If an organization is to consider change, there is the need for new insights and an incentive to do things differently. In a church this is often perceived by the minister, the director of Christian education, or a lay leader. In the case of family education, a family member may first sense its significance; it appears that women recognize this need more readily than men. Whoever articulates this concern in a church must have a vision that something can happen and the will to believe that it can be done.

In a recent survey of Family Life Education in American Baptist churches, it was found that ministers who have had clinical pastoral training and/or post-seminary training are more apt to sense a need for family education in the church programming. The survey states that actual planning for family life education is done by laity, more than the minister, in churches where lay persons have been trained in Parent Effectiveness Training, marriage enrichment, or family enrichment. As more laity assume planning, the activity of family life education rises.[1] Otherwise, where pastors become aware and are trained in the growth process, they have encouraged laity to receive training in all forms of enrichment: parent, marriage, family, and self. The laity serve as leaders and do most of the work in these situations. As enrichment forms become part of a church's program, the survey states that the process encourages churches to be more active among its families. This was found to be true in both large and small communities. The aspirations of American Baptists surveyed imply that:

- churches want help in identifying the needs of families to which they may respond;
- churches need training opportunities for local planners of family life education, enabling them to create programs that will meet the family life needs they have identified in their congregations;
- churches want help in developing intentional intergenerational experiences;
- churches need skill training opportunities in designing and leading intergenerational educational experiences.[2]

It seems apparent that people in churches want help in fostering the growth of their most important human system—the family.

Introducing the Concept

One of the first tasks of an interested parish is to establish priorities for family education in the religious education and pastoral care programs of the church. For many parishes this means reeducating boards and committees, as well as the congregation at large, to the importance of such a ministry, to the need for budgeting money, and to expected differences when compared with the traditional modes of education within the church. Family education "cuts across" age groups and changes the structure of peer-oriented programs of religious education. It emphasizes a systems approach to learning and change, as opposed to an individual approach within peer groups. This is a new concept within church structures; so organizational change needs to be considered.

It is helpful for the leaders and a small ad hoc group of interested persons to begin reading and exploring the family life publications emerging from church presses. Many popular magazines and professional journals print material which is relevant to the needs of family life. An ad hoc committee might establish guidelines for the kind of information needed, might share in the reading, and could produce succinct study papers (of two to three pages) related to the need. These materials could be reviewed by ongoing groups in the congregation: church school classes, parent groups, women's circles, Bible study groups, youth groups, diaconate boards, and prayer groups. The minister could also proclaim this importance from the pulpit. The Family Service Association of America has excellent playlets about concerns of family life[3] which stimulate discussion and concern for the facilitation of family nurture. Data collectors (questionnaires) can also be circulated among family members to gather information (see Appendix A for sample); it is wise to circulate them among all age groups to gain a wider perspective on needs. Collated data can then be used to show interests and reveal the need for family enrichment. Family Clustering, Inc. has a filmstrip and cassette tape (available on a rental basis) about that mode of enrichment for orientation purposes.[4] Consultants are also available from Family Clustering, Inc. for assisting a congregation to be oriented to this need, as well as for helping to introduce actual models. A few denominational judicatories have hired persons to assist churches in meeting the concern for family education.

Another means of stimulating consideration of family enrichment is to sponsor a weekend retreat for families of the parish, including families of those persons in positions of leadership and power. An authentic family retreat is one in which all the family members are together and is facilitated by experienced leaders. Sometimes a one-day event for families is held to motivate further consideration; these opportunities provide understanding for the term "family enrichment" at a time when few persons have experienced education with family groups. Both the United Church of Canada and American Baptist Churches of the U.S.A. have experimented with clergy family clusters to expose clergy to the concept of their own family's enrichment and to increase the awareness to this opportunity for the congregation.

The question is asked sometimes how families are motivated to participate in enrichment activities; experience has shown that families are often ready to do so, but it is the church structure which prohibits it. After hearing of Family Clusters for the first time, one mother exclaimed: "Thank goodness; we have been waiting for this for a long, long time." A Roman Catholic mother, whose children had attended parochial schools, said, "In the long, dark tunnel of religious education, Family Clusters are the first bright light I've seen." Usually a church can recruit families for a short-term event where they are exposed to experiences which will offer them further growth in family education. If a short term pilot experience is held, it provides an opportunity for a parish to try a new mode of education without committing itself to a long-range program. The advantages of such a trial program are:

- it has a beginning and a termination time;
- it is often seen as temporary; therefore, it is less threatening to the status quo;
- it can be evaluated and the data information used for long-range plans;

- it enables people to become acquainted with the purposes and program which are helpful for promoting long-range plans;
- it helps an organization to determine ways it might wish to modify family enrichment for use in ongoing programs

Setting Priorities for Family Education

After a congregation, or organization, determines that the need for family education exists and obtains some data for verification, the committee (or board) responsible for the care and education of families needs to develop some basic, overarching purposes for this emphasis. Many churches have no one responsible for family life, so a new position needs to be created. It appears that the board of Christian education, committee on family ministries, parish counsel, or board of Christian nurture is the most natural place to establish such a position. From this point, persons, or a committee, can begin to obtain information concerning the models of enrichment which would best meet the overall purposes of that particular congregation. These people will want to study the various facets of the models, ask questions, and determine the ingredients needed for implementing the desired models. Chapter 4 offers a listing and description of numerous models of family enrichment. An organization may wish to utilize the skills of a consultant in family education to help them consider the necessary issues in choosing a model of family enrichment. Sometimes ready answers cannot be given to questions raised, since there remain many unanswered questions when dealing with a new mode of education. The act of faith and the mode of risking are important at these times! It is helpful to set a time limit (i.e., three months) on the deliberation process, so a decision can be reached within a reasonable time period.

In their consideration of family education, churches often ask, "Does this replace the Sunday church school?" Any form of family enrichment is an alternative form of religious education which offers families the opportunity for choices relevant to their needs and lifestyles. Some families will want enrichment at certain times of their lives; at other times other forms of religious nurture and education will be needed. The family was the prime educator for learning and nurturing in the faith process throughout thousands of years before the advent of the classroom approach to religious education about one hundred years ago. The emergence of family growth groups utilizes the strength of the family unit within a wider support group which might be called "a faith family." In his book *Will Our Children*

Have Faith? John H. Westerhoff III calls for an end to the "schooling-instructional" method of religious education in which schooling is the context and "teaching-learning" the means. He proposes that these need to be replaced with a "community of faith enculturation" method in which the community of faith is the context and interactions between generations are the means of education.[5] This context and type of interaction can be facilitative of caring and loving, which are at the heart of religious growth and maturity. One cluster leader wrote:

> Our Family Cluster is a covenant community. All members . . . entered into a voluntary commitment to participate for two and one-half hours per week for ten weeks. I have watched in our Family Cluster as children and adults share feelings and love as could happen nowhere else in our society: families experiencing the joy of being together.

Family enrichment is also different from the popular intergenerational approach of church schools. In such programs, a person from one age group (usually those age six and older) participates in an activity with persons of other generations. This is enrichment and education across generations which brings awareness and caring into action. The concept of family enrichment encompasses an intergenerational approach because of the age variance in families. It also is based on the strength and emotional cohesion of the family as a system, thereby utilizing those elements for their impact on interaction and perceptions.

Some elements to be considered in the establishment of family education are:

- the general theological orientation of a parish;
- general perceptions regarding religious education and expectations of the educational ministry;
- the habitual ways change is exerted within the organization;
- the establishment of a budget for implementation of family enrichment programs;
- the recruitment of leaders, with allocation of time and budget for their use;
- the utilization of a public relations approach for widespread exposure within the congregation;
- the approval and sanction of the staff, church board, and "the power people" of the organization.

Recruitment of Families

There are a number of ways to recruit families for enrichment programs. Most congregations have families who would appreciate such an experience, so it is helpful to begin by advertising that family enrichment is available for families who apply for further information. Larger parishes may need to recruit through some sort of selection process, through a couples' class, a marriage enrichment group, a parents' group, or some other specific clientele. The willingness of families to apply often depends on the general mores of the congregation and the trust persons have in the church as a whole. If a parish is open to growth models and interpersonal events, family enrichment will probably be accepted more readily. A church unused to such will need more cultivation and encouragement for self-disclosure and risk taking. Families in churches within small communities may not be attracted at first to such a model, due to their need for protective privacy in a smaller community or due to ethnic mores or parochialism in general. Family Clusters have been used in all types and sizes of parishes: the small rural parish, the town parish, the inner city parish, the large suburban parish, the campus parish.

For many people, the word "family" automatically means two parents and children. Today, family sociologists have enlarged that definition to mean that "a family is composed of any persons who live in relationship (usually in one household)." Using this broader definition, a family is any kind of household unit or familial grouping; clusters have incorporated all styles of family living. They have had one-parent families with children, three-generation families, couples without children, blended families of two adults with children from past marriages who have chosen to become a third family unit. Also, clusters have successfully incorporated single persons who live alone, persons who live together, homosexuals, as well as families with foster children, retarded or handicapped members, or aging persons. Because the nature of planning emanates from the persons in the clusters, any type of family unit can be a part of a cluster and be a recipient of the support and care of this covenant community.

A congregation may need to decide if it will minister only to the families of its active membership or if it will include others. It appears that there are many families in today's society who covet such an experience, for whom the church no longer has meaning in their lives. One woman testified on a radio broadcast: "The church ministered to us (with Family Clusters) and now we're giving more time to the church—it was a turning point in our growth experience in that church."[6] A number of persons have returned to the "mainstream" of the church through cluster participation which helped them to sense their importance to the congregation. Churches can also include in a cluster families new to the church fellowship; this provides a means of becoming acquainted and finding new opportunities for support and concern. One young couple testified:

> As new members of the church, we found cluster an excellent way to establish new friendships and become a part of the church fellowship. Personally, we each felt that the active interpersonal relationships we experienced with other group members of all ages helped us to be more outgoing and positive in our outlook toward life.

Another means for recruiting families is in conjunction with a counseling center, mental health clinic, social service agency, parochial school, or the like. This type of cluster has been started by several agencies on the North American continent to provide a support group for families who have completed counseling or who need a change from the counseling routine. The mixture of functioning families with one or two dysfunctioning ones provides a catalytic approach whereby all the family units have meaningful growth experiences together. Such a support group, guided by highly skilled leaders, is a tremendous way to share faith and care with families who are "hurting" but who may not be exposed to a congregational support system. One social worker of a large agency commented:

> . . . I think that in terms of nurture, support, caring and acceptance the . . . family received more help and healing in those sessions of the Cluster than they would have received in five months of individual service at my agency.

This type of cluster combination is the sharing of social action at one of its most strategic places in society. Luciano L'Abate states that four types of families are "unenrichable":

1. families in extreme crisis;
2. very chaotic families;
3. uncooperative families;
4. families with entrenched symptoms.[7]

It is unusual for any one of these four types to desire or to consider being in a cluster. If a leader does meet with a family which manifests some of the above characteristics, it is best to tell them that cluster would not meet their needs.

Contracting with Families

Contracting is an outward manifestation of an inner commitment; it is important to receive commitment to a growth program from each member of a family. It is a new experience for families as a complete unit to agree to belong to such a group. It is my belief that a leader must be "sold" on the contractual mode of invitation, as well as have a clear perception of what it is he or she is asking families to do. It is also helpful that the family members perceive the leader as a person who is authentic and legitimate with such a request.

Family contracts are best made in the family's home with each individual present, so each has an understanding of what is expected of the individual and family unit within cluster membership. A family contract includes:

1. The purpose of the cluster,
2. Times of sessions and expectations for attendance,
3. Number of sessions to be held,
4. The level of interaction expected,
5. Roles of the leaders,
6. Expectations of family members,
7. Other important considerations as they may be developed by the leaders or the family.

Sometimes one family member will not wish to participate for a variety of reasons, but I feel it is important to emphasize the need for the *complete* family to be present. A teenager may have a reason for not participating, based on his or her own need for more independence from the family unit. If a spouse does not want to attend, there often is a deeper reason behind the reluctance which may foster polarization within the marriage relationship. Often a father/husband is away on business trips but would like to belong to a group; this person is encouraged to attend when possible; periodic absences are included in the family contract. My experience has been that families which do not experience unanimity in the decision to contract and to attend do not put a high priority on clustering. I recall going to the home of a one-parent family to contract. In this family, consisting of the mother and five children of whom three were males in late adolescence, the sixteen-year-old male (and second child) held the power of decision making. He determined which persons of the family would attend clusters and which would not; moreover, those who attended were to be the females! We two leaders were not unified in our decision of whether or not to accept a partial family. The "women" of the family decided to attend, but during the contracted time they were irregular in attendance, usually tardy, and finally dropped out by the sixth session. This experience convinced me of important elements in contracting:

- The leaders should be unanimous about their decision as to the acceptance of a partial family and bring this concern before the entire cluster.
- A family member who decides for the group should be confronted in regard to whether that individual should have the right to answer for all family members.
- Family members need to be aware of what they are contracting "out of" if they decide to stay out of the cluster.
- Usually a partial family commitment means partial commitment on the part of those who decide to attend; leaders need to deal with this ambiguity when it comes up in the cluster sessions.
- A powerful family member can control the family in subtle ways which are often at the "unawareness level."
- This type of power control is indicative of control facets evidenced in other family relationships.
- A family usually needs to contract for a minimum of ten to twelve sessions in order for change to be introduced within the family system.
- A family is not seriously "damaged" by being refused membership in a cluster.

During the home visit, each person, no matter how young, should be asked to commit him or herself. In some churches families sign a written contract or write out their agreements to share with other cluster families. A leader needs to deal with each family on an individualized basis in regard to contracting and the response of family members, for each person will perceive differently his or her investment in the contractual process. Some persons have suggested that contracting is like "holding a club" over a family, which can produce resistance and guilt. Sometimes the semantics of the word "contract" provoke anxiety; so other words can be used interchangeably: "covenant," "pact," "agreement," "ground rules." If the covenant/contract is made with all family members together, each having an opportunity for input, there seems to be little resistance or guilt. Such an agreement provides security and commitment for family members in a group process. It also provides a model of commitment for family members to use among themselves in regard to decisions, assignment of chores, and other areas of family life.

If a parish has more than one cluster, the decision needs to be made as to which family goes into which cluster. My experience is that this decision is more easily made by the leaders who have a grasp of the total context than by the families involved. Sometimes families request that they be in a certain cluster, and that request may be honored when feasible. Three "rules of thumb" seem to be important for dividing families into clusters:

1. The ages of children and youth
   American children are not used to being the only members of their age span in a group; so we try to match similar ages of children/youth.
2. Times the complete family can attend a cluster session
   Families have such a myriad of activities among their members that sometimes there is only one free time in a week when all can be present.
3. The blending of one family's characteristics with another family's features
   Sometimes one family will possess a trait from which another family could benefit if they were in the same group; an attempt is made to match families' characteristics as well as to provide contrast in family styles.

If a church has only one cluster group, then it will have all the families recruited in that one group. Sometimes the fear is expressed that clusters might become cliques. Since there is a termination time to clusters in the contract and since persons are grouped according to the aforementioned criteria, this is not apt to occur.

The Beginning Cluster Sessions

The first time the families come together is strategic to the future life of the cluster. The families will have already contracted to be in a cluster for a number of weeks; so a high degree of motivation is present. The cluster is made up of families who appear to "blend" together, led by two leaders who have learned some of the skills important in the leadership of an intergenerational, family-system-based growth group. (See chapter 6 regarding training of leaders.)

The usual facets of group building are utilized in these early sessions: songs, games, exercises for becoming acquainted by individuals and by families, discussion of expectations, contracting, and the start of the first unit of study. Some differences between group building in a peer group and in an intergenerational group are:

- Activities need to be paced to the interest of differing age groups;
- A change of pace can be introduced approximately every ten minutes;
- Concrete activities need to be utilized, i.e., writing out directions, simplifying directions, using three-dimensional materials, using body movement, etc.,
- Songs, games, activities, and conversation should be adaptable, and some should be used for the benefit of the youngest children during each session;
- An intergenerational "mix" needs to be assured;
- Positive affirmation needs to be introduced for each family unit.

An essential part of the first session is the introduction of a group contract between the families and with the leaders. This contract is different from the individual family contracts made in each home before the cluster began. The group contract is a commitment of each person and each family to the process of the group's functioning. The elements of the cluster contract are discussed in the next section of this chapter.

When starting a new family cluster, it is usually helpful to begin with a unit on communication. Since the families are new to each other and the "trust level" of the group is low, a suggested unit is needed. First, the esteem level is considered, and persons are encouraged to share positive ways of appreciation and respect for every individual within the family. Communication is a vital force for group building, as well as a crucial element in the family system. Before persons or systems can consider any content topic, they need to be aware of how and what they are communicating. Functions of communication begin with the awareness level of differences and the uniqueness of each person in the group. The acts of communication are included, i.e., clear speaking, listening and reflecting, ownership of feelings, congruency between verbal and nonverbal messages, methods of giving and receiving feedback, and the importance of affection and touching within the communication process. Families are encouraged to consider ways they want to change and to contract for the attempt to change within time limits. With these communication sectors there are exercises available from many resources which can be modified for use with all age groups. The communication skill which is utilized first and the type of exercise chosen will depend on the nature of the cluster group. The length of time given to each skill differs for various groups according to the acceptance of the members toward new patterns of behavior, the trust level of the group, the force utilized by the "power people" in the group with response from the leaders, and the point at which various families are in their awareness and practice of each area. These are elements of which leaders need to be aware in deciding what is the next appropriate topic in the cluster. Some groups will be open to risk taking while others will be more "closed" and question each activity. I often watch the play of the preschoolers in the cluster to observe some of the subconscious activity of the group, as young children act out reactions to the feelings experienced before the adults will verbalize their concerns and anxieties. Leaders, who are open to risk, can sometimes make way for such feelings to be expressed through their own examples. This exhibits a kind of behavior which families are encouraged to use: that of being open and honest with one's feelings toward other family members.

An overview of the possible timing for a two-hour session of a cluster follows:

15 min. pre-session activities, i.e., records, free play, meal preparations, interviewing, socializing, writing reactions to pictures, quotes, music, puzzles, "graffiti sheet" for free drawing, etc.

30 min. a sandwich meal, usually preceded by grace—one family often brings dessert for the group, while beverages are usually prepared at the meeting place

20 min. games, recreation, fun, singing

45 min. structured educational experience, centered around the theme of the unit

10 min. evaluation and closure (families can take turns cleaning up).

It can be seen that two and one-half hours would give more leisure to the cluster schedule. Times are set around commuting hours, travel time, bedtimes for the youngest children, and other scheduled events later in the evening.

The Contracting Process Within the Cluster Group

Every new group begins to establish norms for operating, whether they be spoken or unspoken. A contract is a way to help all members of the group feel a sense of empowerment in the establishment of the group's norms. Children's and youths' expectations and contributions are heard seriously and often incorporated into the group's process. At the conclusion of a contracting session one child said, "They really take me seriously here!" Younger persons are often the first to recognize when the contract is broken. The process of contracting becomes the glue which holds the family subsystems together; therefore, it is a task which every cluster group must undertake.

The elements of a cluster contract are:[8]

1. *The purpose for which the group is established.* The purpose has usually been established by the sponsoring organization to which the families have concurred in their individual contracting.

2. *The expectations of the participants and the leaders.* Expectations are sometimes brought out in the home visits. Further expectations can be recorded by the group on newsprint, and all should be displayed before the group. Children can draw pictures or cartoons. The leaders may wish to collate the expectations before the second session to use in discussing which ones are realistic or which will come later in the cluster life. The leaders might share their expectations of each other and of the group via the "fishbowl" technique where certain designated persons sit in the middle of a group and discuss specific concerns while others listen.

3. *Stated parameters for the group are explained.* Information about the room in which the group meets, rules for such, times of meeting, the number of sessions to be held, tasks which need to be assigned, etc., are all discussed.

4. *The manner in which decisions will be made in the group.* Discuss the various methods which may be used—i.e., majority vote, consensus, leadership decision, or some others. Some groups spend much time on this process while others decide quickly; much depends on the economy of decision making established within the various families.

5. *The kinds and degree of interaction among members in the group.* Because of the intimate nature of the family, affection and caring shown between members become important elements within the dynamics of a cluster.

Another interaction around which to contract is the issue of discipline. When a child is disturbing someone else, what is to be done? Many parents appreciate the assistance of others in the discipline process, while some parents are not used to seeing their children disciplined by others in their presence.

Interactions related to learning tasks are also important to have expressed, i.e., slow learning, varied contributions from many age groups, dislike and anxiety in learning tasks, a facilitating environment for learning, etc.

6. *The method for change or renegotiation of the contract.* A contract should be flexible, open to change, and in process during the life of the group.

7. *Celebration of the commitment made together.* A variety of ways may be used to formalize each person's acceptance of the contract: signing with names, handprints, footprints, shoe prints, or symbols. A song, prayer, cheer, or appropriate expression may then be used for celebration by the total group.

It is important to start the concept and procedure of contracting in the first session (through point #3 listed above), continue in the second session (which takes the most time with points #4, 5, 6 above), and finalize it in the third session (continue with unfinished details through point #7 above). Stories[9], songs, and games[10] can be used to introduce the importance of each person to the group and ways to help their growth. They also help to keep the interest of the group when the longer, less interesting segments are covered. These informal activities highlight the concepts of care, the difficulty in doing things together, the need for each person to be heard, the importance of having ground rules, etc.

If contracting drags, it is often due to the dynamics of a particular family or subgroup; this needs to be clarified before the group moves on. Whenever a group has difficulty over an area of concern and refuses to contract about it, that area becomes a point of friction between individuals and families in the group. Usually the same friction appears time after time to consume the energy and learning possibilities of the group; members come to view it with anger and disgust. Leaders need to be responsive to such frictions and use techniques to surface and resolve conflict creatively. Such techniques are often taught in an experiential workshop on conflict resolution. (See chapter 6 on leadership.) It sometimes helps for the leaders to first share their feelings and anxieties about such a concern via the "fishbowl" technique. Then others can be encouraged to join the "fishbowl." This may help the group to open up in regard to the feelings related to the original point of friction omitted from the contract; such a process provides open sharing from which reconsideration of the situation may take place. In turn, this kind of experience provides a learning situation from which families can learn to deal with conflict. Most church populations are known to avoid conflict; so cluster groups usually do not face such problems until their third or fourth recontracting period.

When all the points of contracting have been covered, it is helpful to review briefly the agreement, ask for comments, and make eye-to-eye contact with each person in the group to assess nonverbal commitment. The process of changing the contract (renegotiation) can be stressed also. If all appear to agree, each person is asked to come up front and sign the contract in the manner chosen. It is helpful to celebrate this conclusion as an important point in the group's development.

The contract is composed on newsprint in front of the group and kept before the group after being signed, as a way of evaluating and appraising the need for change. It also serves to show how a group changes and grows over time which, in turn, is what happens to families. Families can use the contractual mode over many years to work out their areas of commitment. It is a way to agree to new forms of behaviors and the methods to be used in obtaining them. It allows for periodic review by all members of the family and provides a manner in which family members can change together with commitment.

The establishment of a caring process takes time; it is *always* a difficult task; it is often resisted, but *the act of contracting pays off!* Social psychologist Lucinda Sangree states that "Contracting is the 'gem' of the cluster concept."[11] Numerous cluster leaders can testify to its plaudits within the family growth group.

Continuing with the Cluster

After four or five sessions with a communication emphasis, families begin to note areas in which they would like to have other learning experiences. By the fifth or sixth session often they are ready to consider other topics from which to choose. During this time of choosing, families need to have an opportunity to discuss their concerns and questions within their own family unit and put them into priority order. The two most important items on their list can be shared with the cluster group, and others can ask questions and discuss the points. Then each family might submit one topic for the choosing list from which persons in the cluster will vote. I often put up a chart with the choices on it so each person in the cluster can check the one in which he or she is interested. Using a smiling face at one end of the continuum and a frowning face on the other (for each topic) makes it like a game in which children can be interested. From the initials, one can see in which topic the group appears most interested. Sometimes the group will need to make a second vote between two topics which are tied with each other or have similar counts in the voting. In the many family groups with which I've worked, families have always seemed to come quickly to a consensus about the topic they wish to choose, so that a common phenomenon appears to be working.

A curriculum built on people's needs is apt to reach people where they have the strongest feelings and the deepest investment. (See chapter 5 on developing a curriculum within experiential education.) By following an approach based on needs, the families are more ready to learn, as the family system is being touched where response can provoke growth in a behavioral style. Usually cluster groups wish to deal first with more obvious topics of a less threatening nature. In clusters which meet over an extended period of time (fifteen sessions or more), there is apt to be more depth to topics because they are closer to persons' inner needs and concerns, such as beliefs, faith, sexuality, or death. A group needs to develop much trust and intimacy before it will move readily into these areas. In clusters which meet over an extended period of time (twenty-four times or more), I sometimes find there is a desire to return to an earlier theme with more depth. For instance, a cluster which is starting to meet at its third or fourth contractual unit of time (thirty-six sessions or more) will often want to experience a unit again and will do more in-depth work in such. This can be attributed to several reasons; there is more trust in the group, and there is more understanding of the good these skills can bring to the family unit. Also, another stage of development has passed in individual growth, the family system's cycle, and the group process. If a new family has joined the cluster during one of the recontracted periods, repetition of the topic provides an opportunity to introduce them to an area in which the others have had new learnings. Families become teachers to each other. In an enrichment model it is important to help families consider their dreams, wishes, hopes, joys, and sorrows, as well as their problems and concerns. Most families are aware of what areas need improving, but few have had an opportunity to consider their positive attributes. Practically no families have had their strengths affirmed by other families! This provides consciousness of what is important to them, what is going well with them, and what to continue doing with meaning. It is the "good news" for daily living. In a pluralistic society it is important that families be aware of their values and have them affirmed for themselves. This is as true of adults as it is for adolescents and children. One family wrote:

> After two years in Family Cluster, I feel our communication has improved greatly in our family. We have definite family values now, and we are not threatened by other peoples' values or lifestyles like we used to be.

Many families have never considered their strengths and dreams, as complete families. This gives them a new awareness of how they are as a unit and how that unit contributes to their well-being. Also, it is meaningful to have family systems express the strength they see in other families—"strength bombardment" for complete families! With the growing awareness of the importance dreams and wishes play in our inner psyches, we are helping family members develop a strength which will be useful in all manner of situations. It also shows teenagers techniques which will be of importance as they develop new relationships and start new family units.

The number of sessions for a unit of study is different in various clusters and is determined by involvement in the group, periodic evaluation to assess interest, types of intergenerational activities available around an individual topic, appropriateness of the topic as determined by families, and leadership observation. My experience has been that a theme can usually run from four to six sessions, or if interest is keen, from six to eight sessions. Clusters soon develop a thematic and time rhythm which is partially dependent on ages of children, energy levels of high-powered individuals, interest of adolescents, the trust level of persons, ability to cope with differences, and other factors. (Various themes for units are found in chapter 5.)

A Family Cluster should be able eventually to undertake any subject for consideration, but often leaders have "hang-ups" about subject areas, or adult family members have a blockage in considering an area of concern; occasionally a teenager may resist a subject area. Resistance is expressed by some individuals when important issues are kept from surfacing or considered inappropriate to the group. Many persons feel there are certain areas of content which are "religious" and others "secular." Since the Family Cluster Model was initiated as a "religious educational model," some persons do not feel certain topics should be considered because these topics are not within their perception of areas considered "religious." My approach is holistic in that I consider all of life as "religious"; therefore, any areas of question and concern are fraught with religious meaning.

> When pressed to its limits, every psychological question becomes a theological one and every theological question a psychological one.[12]

Religion is concerned with *how* one considers all of the facets of life—not with *what content* one deals. The trend in the behavioral sciences is toward holism—the gestalt[13] of the person in his or her experiencing. To facilitate the religious development of a person, one must deal with the total development of the person; therefore, any question, concern, or subject does have religious significance. It is prudent for leaders to know how to integrate questions and problems of everyday living with religious meaning and scriptural interpretation; so the meaning and traditions of Christianity can be correlated with the daily living of persons.

If a cluster should meet for a longer span of time per session, i.e., six hours once a month, the session may be scheduled in this manner:

30 min.	pre-session activities, plus a structured reacquainting exercise
60 min.	structured educational experience centered around the theme of the unit (relaxing play, "change of pace" activities could be introduced as they are needed)
15 min.	snack time
30 min.	recreation, games, fun
60 min.	second structured experience centered on the same theme
45 min.	eating together, cleanup
60 min.	third structured educational experience centered around the same theme
30 min.	recreation, games, fun—sometimes these can be centered around the theme
30 min.	closing evaluation and closure ritual
6 hrs.	total time

Some clusters have met in isolated mountain areas where persons are able to meet together only once per month for the six hours.

Evaluation and Closure

The response of individuals and family units to participating in a cluster is assessed through evaluative techniques. Sometimes people might be asked to share reactions to the session by telling a feeling they had, a learning, a behavior they want to try. This type of sharing often occurs at the session's conclusion while the group is standing in a circle. Children will enter into the sharing when encouraged to do so at their level of participation. At the conclusion of a six- to eight-session unit, it helps to use a more tangible evaluation through written remarks, response to a questionnaire, taped comments, small group comments collated on newsprint, or in a three-dimensional form made of various building materials. Evaluation can become the stepping-stone for building new units based on the responses of the group members and their present needs. It is helpful to evaluate the year's sessions of clusters, particularly if the same families have stayed together in a group through several renegotiation periods of the contract. This might be accomplished during a complete session through reviewing important elements of past sessions and asking participants to respond with elements they liked best, would like to do differently, and learnings they've experienced. It also helps to ask how people have changed their behavior with participation in a specific unit. At the close of the evaluation time, a period of celebration and ritual can be used incorporating song, movement, Scripture, prayer, chant, or other forms. Celebrations and parties are excellent kinds of closures for a cluster contractual period, and homes provide a different setting for such. Evaluation is important to the sponsoring organization in assessing how the project went and planning for the next steps.

It is important for a group to recognize the need for closure and separation when a cluster is reaching its termination point. This kind of experience is more meaningful when ritualized, so people have an opportunity to be cognizant of their affection and care for one another and to grieve as they go through the separation process. It is also important for those who have experienced trauma in various other kinds of "separation processes" to have the experience of group separation within a faith context. Just as a cluster has a beginning or "birthing" time, so it needs to have a terminating or "dying" time. If a cluster has gone through a renegotiation process for more sessions and one family has chosen not to stay with the group, this provides a graceful ending for that family unit by celebrating their presence within the group. This kind of learning experience is important for all ages to help them be cognizant of a transcendent power which helps them face personal loss and separation; it also assists persons to be in touch with the Spirit/Force within each of us as a part of the security of the universe. This is imperative during a time of rapid social change.

Some people question membership in a cluster for a long period of time. Many clusters go into their second year of programming; one cluster in Rochester continued five years, with different leaders and an occasional change in family membership.[14] How long should one remain in a group? How long does one attend church? How long does one continue education? The human personality is vastly more complex than any subject studied in a course, while the family system brings an intense impact to bear on all of us in life's development. If a Family Cluster is in a state of periodic renewal, a member family can be rejuvenated year after year.

Problems in the Use of the Family Cluster Model

Occasionally churches have utilized this model and have had unsuccessful results, some of which seem to stem from the following problems:

1. *Lack of skilled leadership.*
Family cluster leaders need to possess certain skills to facilitate a cluster in ongoing growth. In addition, leaders should have dealt with their own feelings toward self, others, families, and the in-depth issues of life.

2. *Lack of utilizing the contractual mode in family commitment.*
If individuals and families do not contract adequately, their commitment is often of low caliber, which results in lowered morale in the cluster group.

3. *Lack of utilizing experiential education as a means of learning for all participants.*
Through experiential learning, all ages of family members can participate and share feelings and responses at their own level. This insures the active involvement of all ages, as well as satisfaction toward the experience.

4. *Lack of using the group's ideas as agenda.*
The church has often been an institution with "impositional" learning, which makes for dependency, conformity, and misuse of creative capabilities. By using the ideas of the group, the leader helps group members to be more responsible for their own lives.

5. *Lack of understanding as to what is healthy family functioning versus family dysfunctioning*

Family Cluster leaders are not therapists, and sometimes a family has problems which cause it to be dysfunctional. Leaders need to be able to "spot" such families, sort out their feelings toward them, and refer such families to counseling agencies. This also means leaders need to be aware of their own emotional needs, take responsibility for their own feelings, and not use the group for personal coping. Good education has always used techniques which are therapeutic in nature. The chief distinction between Family Cluster education and family therapy is that between promoting growth or alleviating pathology.

6. *A lack of understanding in churches of the attributes of diversity and the need for alternative forms of religious education.*

If the minister and key members of the church feel threatened by the concept of alternative educational forms, then it is difficult to expect support for this or any alternative form.

7. *The influence of the family on each person.*

Each individual has experienced the gamut of human emotions and relationships within some family setting; those influence the subconscious whenever anyone is considering any aspect of family education. This "hidden agenda" permeates and influences what persons do within the context of a family group or the organization as a whole.

In conclusion, it is appropriate to share a few testimonials as to what Family Cluster membership has meant to various ages.

Cluster helps our family in solving problems among us.

—Eleven-year-old child

Before clusters, I felt "dumb," "chicken" about things. People help you here. My voice is just as important as anyone else's. I understand myself more.

—An adolescent female

Last evening we had our first "Family Council" (learned in cluster), and I am quite happy with the results. Our family contract has been drawn up and duly signed; I no longer have to worry about running the family. It now looks like a logical solution to a lot of our family difficulties.

—Mother of three children

On my job, industry causes people to be looked at as things. Cluster is a constant reminder to me that human beings are important in my life.

—A father in an executive position

CHAPTER *4*

Models of
Family Enrichment

Family enrichment is an outgrowth of the group work and human potential movements of the sixties. Both of these contributed experiential techniques, theory, research, and workshop formats which became integrated into many enrichment programs in the seventies. About the same time, Virginia Satir and other family therapists developed nontraditional approaches for working with dysfunctional families; multifamily therapy and family network therapy emerged. Herbert Otto conducted research in 1961 on family strengths, and from that he developed some programs of strength building for family groups. Also, the concept of marriage enrichment for couples was commencing through the work of David and Vera Mace with the Society of Friends (Quakers) and the leadership of Fr. G. Galvo with Roman Catholic Marriage Encounter groups in Spain. Education for enrichment and actualization was under way!

About this time there was also a growing concern for the family as the basic unit of society, which became popularized in the mass media. Pastors, therapists, counselors, and social workers were besieged with the problems and crises of "family breakdown," while the development of support groups was undertaken by divorcees, widows, women and men, homosexuals and lesbians, single parents, the aging, and many others. It seemed to be a time when each kind of group was advocating its cause. It became clear that a preventive approach for family units was needed to cope in a fast-changing world.

What Is Family Enrichment?

With the proliferation of ideas and models, as well as the lack of communication between persons in the enrichment fields, concepts and definitions have not been clarified. There is vagueness and overlapping between many models and persons' perceptions of them. There has been no attempt to delineate between various terms, and many are used interchangeably. Therefore, I have attempted to provide some definitions and meanings to the following terms:

prevention— to avert pathology and dysfunctioning from becoming started;

enhancement—to provide greater value and importance to the goodness (strengths) already inherent in relationships, thereby increasing their productivity;

actualization—to build on the growth effectiveness already existing and to provide momentum for further growth toward increased fullness and wholeness;

growth— to facilitate a person or human system toward greater maturity in functioning.

Whatever term is used, the basic concept implies that there is an ongoing unit of persons in functioning relationships which can be strengthened and facilitated to move toward more integration, maturity, and wholeness. The biblical term *shalom* implies this, and the New Testament Scriptures affirm "abundant living" through the teachings of Christ. The field of enrichment interfaces with the biblical interpretations of Christian living.

There are five basic types of enrichment which enhance family living:

1. *Individual* enrichment for one person to enhance individual growth;
2. *Parent* enrichment for one or both parents to facilitate parent/child relationships;
3. *Marriage* enrichment for the husband/wife couple to enhance their adult marriage relationship;
4. *Intergenerational* enrichment for two or more persons of various ages to intensify their relationship with each other;
5. *Family* enrichment for the complete family, as a relational system living within a household unit, to facilitate the total family relationship.

The last one deals with all of the others, plus the system of the family.[1] The systems approach to relationships is more than the sum of its parts or sub-parts. It utilizes an exponential factor inasmuch as each family member influences all other members. This happens in a myriad of ways and is explained mathematically by the following formula:

I = interactions

N = number of individuals in family

$I = N^2 - (N-1)$

i.e., with four individuals in a family

$I = 4^2 - (4-1)$

I = 13 interactions each time the four individuals are together.

From the pattern of interactions in a family, relationships are developed between all of the persons. These are the patterns by which the individuals develop relationships with the outside world as well as cope with all of the problems thrust upon them.

Family enrichment uses the strength of the family unit as a teaching force toward growth and actualization. This approach assumes that younger family members can bring change and growth to a family unit as well as can older family members. In order to introduce new learnings into a family system, it appears that an educational environment which incorporates each person within that system has more intensity and faster learning processes within today's world. A family enrichment model is authentic to the system of the family when it uses the dynamics of the complete family system as its base.

Categories of Family Enrichment Models

Models of family enrichment share many of the same characteristics, yet each has its own unique factors or clientele which it serves. Many have not developed a philosophical base nor determined what theoretical foundations contribute to them. Unfortunately, many persons in the church use advertising slogans, "word of mouth" suggestions, or certain theological connections to choose models rather than the philosophy out of which the models are developed. Categories into which I've classified the various models are:

1. *The Family Growth Group*

This type of model uses the group process as an inherent part of interaction and growth to strengthen the family; therefore, *inter*-family interaction is as important as *intra*-family interaction. An underlying philosophy is that individuals and systems change under the influence of the group, while a basic theological tenet is that individuals and systems need a "support" community/group of love and faith.

2. *Family Skill Models*

This type of model uses skill training and practice as an educational thrust with the complete family system. The skills may be taught to separate families or within a group. An underlying philosophy is that family systems function better when certain skills are used, and individuals are more productive citizens as a result of living in a healthily functioning system.

3. *Family-Based Models for Religious Indoctrination*

This type of model is based on the premise that the learning of certain religious concepts is essential to a faith developmental system, and that these concepts are more forcibly learned within the emotional context of the family. These models use specific didactic content developed from theological premises of a particular belief process. An underlying philosophy is that religious faith is more forcibly taught within the family unit.

4. *Family-Based Models for Recreation and Socializing*

This type of model is built on the premise that families can be strengthened through sharing fun and recreation together in a spirit of fellowship. No specific educational goals are established nor structured program presented, so the format and learnings are random and informal.

None of these categories includes the communal household or groups of families living together under one roof in intentional communities. Information about such groups can be obtained elsewhere. Addresses for information concerning each model are found in Appendix B.

Family Growth Groups

The Family Cluster is a name both Herbert Otto and I have used for enrichment models with differing facets.

1. The Family Cluster, as I have developed the model, is a group of four or five complete family units which contract to meet together periodically over an extended period of time for shared educational experiences. They provide mutual support for each other, learn skills which enhance living within the family, and celebrate their beliefs and life together. A "family" may be any person or persons who live in relationship, so a cluster encompasses any type of family, i.e., a one-parent family, a couple without children, a single person, a three-generational family, a nuclear family, etc. The model has two leaders

who serve as facilitators to individuals, to families, to simulated families, and to the group as a whole. Training is available for leaders. The complexity of the dynamics of the model makes it one of the most sophisticated family enrichment models.

2. The Family Cluster, developed by Herbert Otto, is a group of three to five families who meet regularly (number of sessions is determined by the group) in a climate of intimate sharing and caring for the purpose of actualizing individual and family potential. They generally share similar aims, goals, and values and may share specific family functions and services. No attempt is made to consider problems of the "negative" facets of family life; rather the emphasis is on positive attributes and strengths. Leadership is shared by members of the group in whatever way they prefer.

3. *The Family Actualization Model*, developed by Anne Lee Kreml. The central purpose of this model is to help functioning families understand and work through family conflicts in everyday living. This practice can result in increased sharing and deepened relationships so that the family becomes more "actualized." Led by a highly skilled leader, the model was developed for a small group of families within a church setting. They meet together weekly for eight times in two-hour sessions, as well as two weekends in a retreat setting. The author's rationale and theological orientation are described in her Master of Divinity thesis.[2]

4. *The Family Camp*, developed by Ed Branch of Canada. This model is a combination of marriage enrichment and family enrichment, held in a camp setting for one week. The major emphasis is on the marriage relationship, and children observe their parents valuing and enjoying their marriage as they work through their problems and concerns. The premise assumes that as the parents model growth in marital relationship, this provides the most strategic building block in family relationships. Such relational behavior has a stronger impact on children than parenting behaviors, which are more often observed in families. Adults and children are separate much of the time but come together once a day in a family activity. There are two leaders for the fifteen couples and their family units.

5. *The One-Parent Family Camp*, developed by the Five Oaks Conference Center of the United Church of Canada. This week-long, residential camping program has been in operation since the fifties and is specifically geared to the one-parent family. A highly skilled therapist works with the parents in a morning group session while the

children are in peer groupings. Occasionally there are family activities during the week. The guiding purpose is to provide nurturance for the single parent and skilled therapeutic intervention in the family system when needed; this, in turn, leads to a sense of freedom and growth for the family.

6. *Family Weekend,* developed by Ted Bowman. This experiential model, adapted from my Family Cluster Model, was developed for a weekend camp setting to promote the enhancement of family strength and potential. Planned for six to eight families, members rotate between individual, family, or total group activities. The Weekend was developed for families in counseling with the Family and Child Services of Charlotte, North Carolina, in conjunction with functioning families from church-related agencies in the area; this provides a linkage between counseling services and family enrichment. The groups are led by highly skilled, professional staff who use therapeutic intervention when needed. A training component was introduced in 1975 so professionals could utilize the model in their agencies.

7. *Family Enrichment Weekend,* developed by Carl Clarke, Russell Wilson, and June Wilson for Methodist congregations. These weekend programs of three to four sessions are usually held for twelve families in a camp or retreat setting. The program uses a highly structured manual composed of exercises aimed to facilitate family members in affirming the value and worth of one another. Couples are trained to serve as leaders through weekend in-service training with another couple.

8. *Family Enrichment*, developed by the Character Research Project of Union College, Schenectady, New York, for the National YMCA. This short program works within the dynamics of ongoing yearly groups of Indian Guides, Maidens, Princesses, and Trail Blazers—all parent-child programs of the Y. One parent works with a child with structured activities during the three sessions, each with a different topic. A cassette tape and activity sheets provide the needed leadership, along with a leader's manual. Periodic training is held in various parts of the country.

Family Skills Models

1. *The process model of Virginia Satir* is well known, and she conducts workshops and intensive seminars of varying length. Satir states that she has no name for her model:

What describes it best is a process approach based on communication and self worth concepts, working toward growth and change. This is aimed toward helping people to be equality oriented (instead of only hierarchially oriented), uniqueness directed (instead of only conformity directed), and holistic understanding (instead of only linear thinking).[3]

She often works with functioning families and uses various techniques within simulated families, dyads, triads, the total group, or with a family unit in front of the group. Satir, as the leader/therapist, determines which technique is used. The training component consists of observation of her modeling, didactic interpretations, and questions.

> The most important thing I try to teach is how to become more fully human, and for the practitioner to be able to use him or herself in the same way in the interest of those he contracts to help.[4]

2. *Peoplemaking Through Family Communication,* developed by Joseph Roberts and Jan Berry for the National Communication Skills Center (a project of the National Board of YMCAs), is an experiential learning program of six sessions, each three hours in length, based on the theory of Satir as found in her book, *Peoplemaking.* Geared to a group of six families, it helps family members discover their uniquenesses, self-worth, points of conflict, and enjoyment of each other—which all lead to family growth. Each group has one leader who follows a structured program developed in an extensive manual. The manual is available through participation in one of the leader training workshops held throughout the country by the National Family Skills Communication Center.

3. *Filial Programs,* developed by Bernard Guerney and colleagues at the Family Consultation Center of Penn State University, are short-range programs developed for skill training in interpersonal competency between

children (ages 5 to 10 years) and their parents

or

adolescents and their parents.

The program for parents of younger children trains them, through play therapy, to be more effective in child-rearing skills, child-management behaviors, and in meaningful relationships with their children. The program for parents and adolescents uses the age groups together to help them learn to express themselves in specific, constructive ways, as well as to respond to each other with empathy and understanding; these behaviors resolve conflicts and problems more readily. Leaders are professionals who use the book *Relationship Enhancement*[5] and skill training sheets. A three-day training sequence is offered periodically by staff from the center.

4. *The Family Enrichment Program,* developed by Luciano L'Abate and associates at Georgia State University, Atlanta, Georgia, is a series of six to ten sessions for the individual family (classified as being "non-clinical") to explore new possibilities of relating among their family members. Preprogrammed, structured exercises provide opportunity to increase self-awareness, other-awareness, proficiency in communication skills, and problem solving. Programs have been developed for various kinds of families and come in both simple and complex forms; so either can be chosen to fit the cognitive, educational, and socioeconomic levels of the family. This model is part of a degree program within the university for enrichment and therapy training for professionals, paraprofessionals, therapists, and educators. It is based on the concept that enrichment provides rich experiences at the beginning, middle, or conclusion of therapy; it, therefore, serves as an adjunct to therapy. An extensive evaluation and research process is included.

5. *The Community Family Workshop,* developed by Laurent Roy, approximately ten sessions in length, is for parents, children, or any person interested in learning and changing their "family scripting." Built on the TA concept of scripting within the family (which is passed from one generation to another), the workshop helps individuals to consider:

positional dimensions (where you presently are)
directional dimensions (where you are headed if you keep going in the same direction)
procedural dimensions (what might be done)

The professional leader helps an individual "restructure" his or her present family through family sculpting, so that the person can see how the dynamics look and decide how to effect change. The process is based on movement of the individuals through family sculpting, rather than discussion of feelings. It is also used with children and families with problems of abuse, alcoholism, etc.

6. *Family Check-Up,* developed by Dawn Simon for use with Family and Child Services of Greater Seattle, Washington, is a one-day checkup held with four or five families to assess their strengths, to consider areas of needed change, and to enjoy each other. Family members fill in a questionnaire at the beginning of the day and again at the conclusion to check on improvements in self-awareness, communication, and caring. The leaders are social workers associated with the agency.

7. *Understanding Us,* developed by Patrick Carnes for Interpersonal Communications Programs, Inc., of Minneapolis, is a preventive educational program for a family with children six years or older. In four sessions a family develops "The Family Map" to help each member view his or her position in the family, as well as what each contributes and what each receives in the family. Another activity, "The Dependency Cycle" gives each family member an understanding of how he or she is constantly changing and that impact on the family. The content lends itself for inclusion of a liturgy from a religious setting. *Understanding Us* is designed for participation by eight to fifteen families who work both in a group and at home. Leaders are encouraged to be trained in two-day workshops held periodically throughout the United States.

8. *The Family Class/Workshop* was developed by Re-Evaluation Counseling of Seattle, Washington. Counseling with a family in this setting is based on the theory and understanding of Re-Evaluation Counseling.[6] The theory assumes that each person is born with tremendous intellectual potential, natural zest, and lovingness. These qualities become blocked and obscured in persons as the result of accumulated "distress experiences" in the growing stages (i.e., fear, hurt, loss, pain, anger, embarrassment, etc.). When adequate emotional discharge (i.e., crying, trembling, raging, laughing, etc.) can take place, the person is freed from the rigid patterns of behavior and feeling which have been left by the hurt. The basic loving, cooperative, intellectual, zestful nature is then free to operate so the person is able to *reevaluate* his or her situation for action. The process used is peer cocounseling between persons of all ages and of any background, whereby they exchange effective help with each other to free themselves from the effects of any past distress experiences.

In the Family Class or Workshop, a skilled leader works with the individuals in a family, aiding them to discharge and to reevaluate patterns of family interaction. At the same time, the group provides the needed support and affirmation during and after the discharging. Classes and training in Re-Evaluation Counseling are held throughout the United States and the world.

9. *Familylabs,* developed and led by Monica Breidenbach and Margot Hover, is a series of six to ten sessions presented weekly or through a weekend. The program is composed of structured exercises around the goals: role sensitivity, clarifying value systems, and increasing sensitivity to family identity. Families work alone in their

own units. The leaders also present family-based programs in religious awareness and rituals, through their consulting agency.

Family-Based Models for Religious Indoctrination

1. *Family-Centered Programs,* developed by the Religious Education Department of the Glenmary Home Missioners in Nashville, Tennessee, are Roman Catholic in theology and in liturgy and are developed annually around seasonal religious themes which emphasize the scriptural meanings and history of the themes. The highly structured manual can be used by an untrained leader with a group of families or used by individual families in their homes. There are six to twelve sessions for different themes, culminating with an all-parish liturgy using the Eucharist. Since the Religious Education Department ministers to parishes in Appalachia, the material is particularly suited to the small rural parish.

2. *Families,* developed by Maureen Gallahger of Green Bay, Wisconsin, and produced by Paulist Press, is a commercial program available for a five-year span, in yearly sequences, built around annual themes which are based on Roman Catholic theology and liturgy. During the two-hour sessions, children, youth, and adults are divided into peer groups and study a common theme under the leadership of volunteers. A short family sharing session for each family follows, concluding with a family service of the Eucharist. Any number of families can participate in a sequence although no formal commitment is made with families. An expensive slide-tape set is used with adults which presents excellent theoretical interpretations of the religious and psychological development of persons. An explicit coordinator's manual can also be obtained.

3. *Family Learning Teams,* developed by Mercedes and Joseph Iannone in Alexandria, Virginia, is composed of twelve to fifteen families of a parish within geographical proximity who wish to develop a faith emphasis at home by assuming responsibility for the religious education of family members. Roman Catholic in origin and theology, the concept is rooted in small units of inter-generational groupings which are the foundation of religious education in the parish. Emphasis is on support structures for families within the sacramental catechesis. The parents usually develop twenty weekly instructional programs for peer groups of children and youth. Once a month all families gather together to share in an activity and the liturgy of the Eucharist. Each family is expected to be a "steward" to the others by volunteering their homes,

time, and talent. Training of teachers for the peer groupings is sponsored by the local parish, while periodic seminars are held to train coordinators to develop the concept in their parishes.

4. *Family Weekend Experience* was developed by Jack and Marcia Byington for Worldwide Marriage Encounter. This commercial kit of materials contains sample materials and information needed for up to twenty families to spend a weekend together. The main thrust is toward strengthening family life through a series of explicit activities regarding uniqueness, roles, intimacy, and helping each other. The kit includes a *Team Manual* with directions for organizing a weekend, a *Team Training Cassette,* and materials to use with families.

5. *The Mishpacha,* developed by Dov Peretz Elkins, is an adaptation of Sawin's Family Cluster to fit a Jewish religious style through the use of prayers, rituals, education, and the creation of "community" within the Jewish tradition. There are two leaders for a group. In synagogues where it has been used, congregations have felt that it had tremendous potential for Jewish religious education, for strengthening Jewish family life, and for overcoming alienation among Jewish adherents. Training is available through the events held for Family Cluster training.

6. *The Family "Havurot"* was developed by the Reconstructionist Jewish Movement. This particular type of *havurot* is composed of a small group of families (ten or less) which meet monthly to pursue programs of Jewish education for adults and children, to celebrate, and to provide a surrogate extended family. In peer groupings, persons explore Jewish issues and experiment with the translation of Jewish learnings into styles of living. Occasionally workshop orientation is provided by agencies in various sectors of the United States for those interested in *havurots.*

7. *Operation Family,* developed by John and Milly Youngberg for Seventh-Day Adventist churches, is based on a variety of groupings aimed to spread information about the family, as well as to use short strategies with families. They revolve around family needs, belief values, and life-styles. The manual is a resource collection of materials to be used in whatever way leaders decide: large lecture group, family groups, peer groups, married couples.

8. *Sunday School Plus,* developed by Larry Richards, is a commercial model which uses common curricular themes in the peer groupings of the Sunday school, plus suggestions for families to use the theme at home. The material is evangelical in orientation.

9. *Kits for Parents,* developed by David C. Cook Publishing Company, are commercial kits developed for parents to use for their study and for families to utilize in activities at home. They feature "Family Unity" and "Self-Esteem."

Several other denominational programs have been developed for individual families to use in their homes, among them *The Family Home Evening* of the Church of Jesus Christ of Latter-Day Saints (Mormon); *The Christian Life Home Curriculum* of the Christian Church (Disciples of Christ); *Family Night Program* of the Christian Family Movement (Roman Catholic). Many other single books and resources have been published commercially to use with families in home settings or in group settings. (Some are listed in the Bibliography.) There are also a number of singular programs developed by denominations and other publishing houses for use in vacation church schools, camp settings, retreats, sacramental preparations, and others. It is suggested that contact be made with denominational publishing houses and publishers of religious education material for intergenerational family-based materials.

Family-Based Models for Recreation and Socializing

1. *The Extended Family,* developed by the First Unitarian Church of Santa Barbara, California, encourages groups of families and persons to socialize together and to be involved in activities which are important to each participant; as a result, the care and sustenance would be like that in the extended family. Each group is autonomous in determining time and length of meeting, program, format, etc. The model has been used extensively by Unitarian-Universalist churches across the continent. An Extended Family may have a convener but does not have a leader in the structured sense.

2. *The Family Fun Council,* developed by Ann Kilmer and Herbert Otto, is a program for one day in a local church setting which emphasizes the fun and joy aspects of family life. Written in a brief, mimeographed form, it could stimulate thinking and planning of various activities for family units in the church community. It might also provide "spin-offs" for other activities by stimulating interest and developing motivation.

3. *Family Outings,* i.e., camps, picnics, cycle and boat trips, travel caravans, retreats, backpack hiking, and others, have been developed over the years by denominations, judicatories, local parishes, ecumenical groups, camping and retreat centers, and others. Such programs are usually held out-of-doors in informal settings where

families can participate as they wish. Often presented are interest groups in crafts, nature study, outdoor living, recreation, hobbies, campfire skills, and the like. If didactic discussion is held, it usually is informal and in peer groupings. Leadership is usually volunteer and informal.

Herein it has been attempted to share some of the better-known models within various categories of family enrichment; doubtless, there are more. They will continue to proliferate as the family receives new attention and affirmation in our culture.

> There is every indication that this new movement [enriching of relationships] is in the process of making a significant contribution to marriage and family life, both in the United States and in other parts of the world.[7]

Very few models have had extensive follow-up evaluation of a statistical nature; therefore, there is little to share in how well various models work and what they do. Some research is available on models developed within university settings. As far as I know, there has not been any research of a comparative nature between family enrichment models.

Some churches and synagogues which have committed themselves to a ministry of family concerns have combined several modes of enrichment to present wider alternatives to their family units. This allows families to begin enrichment activities in a less-threatening way and with limited commitment. It also allows an organization to gain time to develop leaders for more sophisticated approaches. For example, a church could begin with a short family enrichment model which might include a structured manual which can be used easily by a relatively unskilled leader. It could then move to an in-depth skill program for families desiring to better interpersonal relations within their family. A third step could be offered for families who want *inter*-family interaction and growth, through a long-range family growth group. Some models appear to be more productive with families at certain stages of family cycle development or with certain kinds of concerns.

In any enrichment model used, one must be clear about the basic philosophy and operation of that particular model. If one modifies a model, one must be prepared to consider different outcomes. Some family enrichment models operate from a needs-based growth process while others use imposed curriculum within a structured format. Families should be recruited, knowing the stated parameters in advance, so that expectations are not uncertain. Sometimes there is waning interest on the part of adolescents, particularly when they are faced with much verbalization which is pedantic or of a moralizing tone. This approach offers lessened power for the adolescents at a developmental period when they desire more power. They may opt to leave the group or rebel in ways the group finds disruptive. When decisions are hierarchically made—that is, by the adults for the youth—this action paves the way for resistance and hostility. It also indicates an adult-oriented group which "expects" children to be a part; it is not a person-centered, family-oriented group which facilitates intergenerational relationships. Moreover, that dictatorial action does not model the kind of behavior which promotes healthy functioning within families. It is helpful to be clear about who makes decisions within a family enrichment group, how, and when so everyone in group membership can have the same understandings.

I can forsee churches hiring consultants to assist families in assessing their skills and needs, utilizing collated data to assist churches in choosing the specific model appropriate for the families in their congregation, and conducting the necessary training. It seems that churches which have used a highly structured model often wish to move into a human relations type of model, while churches which have used the informal social type of model sometimes wish to move into a structured model. It appears that the process of enriching families leads to deeper processes. Desire for growth is at the heart of the Christian gospel. Also to be considered is the fact that various styles of family living provide learnings for the next generation to consider.

Guidelines for Choosing a Model of Family Enrichment

With the proliferation of many forms of family enrichment, it is confusing sometimes to the church educator or administrator as to what to consider in the decision making. Many models have overlapping purposes and techniques, but the worth of any model depends on the people involved in it. Following are some guidelines for the consideration of various models and ways of choosing those most appropriate to your situation:

1. Assess what the family units of the congregation are feeling/thinking/realizing about their situation by obtaining information (data) through:
   • interviewing a representative sample of family members;

- developing a written questionnaire for a large number of families;
- discussing family needs in various sectors of the church, i.e., children's groups, youth fellowships, adult groups.

Do not overlook children and youth in families as a population from which to gain information of a succinct nature. Keep the questions simple. Leon Smith gives examples for obtaining information in *Family Ministry: An Educational Resource for the Local Church.*[8] Try to reach all types of family units.

2. Collate the information gained to see what common threads emerge as indicators of what families would like to do.
3. Draw up some basic, overarching purposes for a family enrichment emphasis in the parish, with a tentative timetable for accomplishing these purposes.
4. Send for samples and details of the family enrichment models which might best fit your purposes and peruse them to match features of a model with family needs. Your own purposes determine what to look for in an enrichment model. Study the rationale and details; ask questions; try some techniques in a family group; obtain the services of a consultant to help in your planning.[9] Set a time limit on your deliberation process so that it does not drag and lose momentum.
5. Determine leadership needs for the enrichment best suited to your purposes. What kind of training/guidance/supervision will be needed? What kind of training is accessible? What needs to be done for recruitment? Start a listing of leadership possibilities. (Many people will lead a family group who will not wish to teach church school.)
6. Determine the budget needed for the enrichment program best suited to your purposes. How will the budget be used? For leaders' manuals? For leadership training? For supplies? For family orientation? For bringing in outside leadership? For purchasing resources?
7. Set time limits for trying an enrichment model, with built-in evaluation devices to give you feedback as to whether it met your purposes—whether families responded and found it helpful—whether it "fits" your church's emphasis in religious education and nurturing.
8. Straddle a gentle line between those who wish to keep the status quo and those who are yearning for support and growth in their family unit. Often the person who resists change in the direction

of family ministries is hurting in his or her own family while hiding behind a mask of hostility and fear.

9. Review the area (chapter 2) on introducing the concern and setting priorities in a parish.

10. Join a support group of persons interested in family enrichment for your own morale and growth in this new field. For names of such persons, send a stamped, self-addressed envelope with your request to Family Clustering, Inc.[10] There are many professionals interested in the family unit in most communities; seek them out and let them know of your enrichment concerns.

Sources of Resistance to Family Enrichment

Herbert Otto states that the first resistance to enrichment models

. . . begins with the inbuilt resistance of the individual to growth and change. Growth involves change, and change is linked with the appearance of the new. With very few exceptions people tend to avoid the new because they have become habituated to the status quo in themselves and others close to them.[11]

There also is tremendous resistance to change by a family system. This is often revealed in statements, such as "Our family does not have problems like that!" . . . "We are getting along OK" . . . "We have no more problems than the next family." Because family life is so privatized and isolated in our culture, many people think most families interact in the way their family does; through observing other families, they would have opportunity to consider other behaviors. Often a rebellious adolescent or child is the most powerful person in keeping a family from consideration of an enrichment experience. Therefore it is important in family recruitment for the leader to visit the home and to have direct contact with everyone in the family. It takes considerable ego strength for a leader to confront a resistant family member in the initial contracting session. Some parents find it easier to pick out an "identified person" in the family upon whom they blame problems and lay the need for counseling. Family systems are very intact, and a leader must have some awareness of this strength when he or she attempts to recruit families.

Because families have no cultural methods of checking on themselves and their interaction, they sometimes feel they cannot admit to this need because it is different behavior from the accepted norms. Most of us grew up where "good families" took care of themselves and solved their own problems. There are some remnants of stoicism and Puritan individualism inherent in our thinking about families.

Moreover, in a culture where medical pathology has such persuasive power, psychological prevention is not considered. We are living in the post-industrial age amidst a social revolution; the concept of planned change and enrichment within human systems is new—emotionally, cognitively, and socially.

The presence of one's complete family, within a group of others, can be often threatening to parents whose children are psychological extensions of themselves. Young children are canny in noting the inner feelings of their parents and sometimes embarass adults with their outbursts of honest exclamation! I was demonstrating with a group of families one time and was introducing myself to three active boys, ages four, six, and seven years. I had asked them their names and ages, so I told them my name and age in return. Immediately the seven-year-old flashed back, in front of the group, "You're not supposed to say that!" When I asked, "Why not?" he said, "My mother never tells anyone her age!" It helps if the leader has a sense of humor, with a light touch, honesty in purpose, and ability to empathize with family members at such a time. The well-placed song, game, story, poem, riddle, dance, or stunt can be helpful when interjected at a strategic spot. Sometimes the parent will approach the leader after the session to discuss the meaning behind the situation, and the leader can help a family begin to delve into a more basic question or concern. Often a child's remark underlies a deeper curiosity about a basic life issue with which a family needs to deal; this sometimes can become a thematic unit for the whole cluster.

Sometimes within the church there is the mystique that "religous persons" should not have problems or at least not talk about them. This attitude carries over to a person's faith stance. When the suggestion is made that a family enter into an enrichment experience, it might appear to the family that it is not only being undermined but its faith stance is being questioned; a double bind is exerted. Risking assumes security; in an era of rapid change and lessening of security, often persons are not able to risk much. Their concept of risking involves the worst happenings of the imagination rather than the realities of renewal and change. Many people would rather be forced to consider change under the pressure of a rebellious child or a departed spouse than to use change as an inbuilt way of renewal.

Church populations, by and large, consider diversity as heretical and incongruent with some forms of theology; therefore, the adoption of alternative forms of religious education is new to many congregations. If the minister and other "power figures" in the church feel threatened by the concept and practice of alternative forms, this also hinders a congregation's willingness to consider forms different from the norms. It may also suggest that a congregation's need is consideration of change process before different modes of education can be accepted.

Sometimes a staff member or lay leader is not perceived as "human"; therefore, there may be resistance to them in the role of the leader when they are open and honest with the group. Often church members hold unreasonable expectations for their leaders, and there might be considerable risk for some leaders in certain parishes to behave openly and honestly, as is sometimes needed in a family group.

Where families have had enrichment experiences, they have appreciated and enjoyed them; the large clientele of such family members is a testimony to the fact that resistance can be met and re-channeled to become an energy force which motivates people toward change and growth.

When families become as important to America as football or firearms, the divorce rate will take a deep plunge, nonreaders will cease to become a national problem, juvenile delinquency will experience drop-outs, and neighborhoods will once again become a place for people of all ages to live together.[12]

CHAPTER 5

Curriculum and Resources
for Family Groups

Traditionally, curriculum has been considered as a prescribed course of study built around a content or subject area and designed by a teacher for a group of students. Most curricula is composed of didactic material with resources primarily being books, writings, and lectures. In experiential education, a curriculum is comprised of expressed needs and expectations of the persons involved in the learning situation. Within a growth group, usually the content deals with the experiences of living which are related to the in-depth issues of personhood. These issues emanate from the core of one's being, i.e., sexuality, birth, death, separation, autonomy, dependence, reconciliation, etc. These elements are the heart of religious experience, and the Scriptures present concepts and truths which provide insight for meaningful living. Since Christianity is a religion of relationships—to self, to others, and to a transcendent God—education for Christianity is learning to live one's life continuously in relation to one's self and to others. All of one's self is integrated and influenced by how one lives. Religious behaviors are those behaviors which help a person to discover and to interpret the meaning of life's experiences to his or her satisfaction. They are usually developed and reinforced within a supportive community, such as a family, a church, a club, or a neighborhood group, through teachings, rituals, and liturgies. The kind of behaviors a person has found to be life nourishing and emotionally sustaining within the family are those one will probably use as a base to give interpretation to life's existence. One of the foremost thinkers in religious education,

Horace Bushnell, has been quoted as saying: "No truth is really taught by words or interpreted by intellectual methods; truth must be lived into meaning before it can be fully known."

When we consider a curriculum for Christian education, we must emphasize a process for living in relationship.

The Model of Family Enrichment Determines the Curriculum

The previous chapter contains categories of numerous models of family enrichment; an individual model determines the content of the curriculum and techniques to be used. The models of socializing and fellowship use no programming nor structured teaching (i.e., the Extended Family Model); so there is no need for manuals or resource books. The models for religious indoctrination follow certain religious beliefs and utilize curriculum and techniques expressive of those beliefs. The family skill models follow certain theories about nurturing families; usually they have an established body of information and a set of skills which are explicitly outlined in a manual. The most difficult models for which to plan are the growth group models, as they infer that the growth of individuals and of family systems is enhanced by the group process; this cannot be programmed in advance. Experiential education is the basis of planning for such a model since experiences are planned from the needs of the group members; therefore, techniques and resource ideas are subject to that guidepoint of the basic philosophy. Many leaders are not used to working within this framework and, therefore, find it difficult and time-consuming. If leaders are not available to function with this kind of model, then another model needs to be chosen. If leaders are not accustomed to working within an experiential framework, their basic approach would need to be considered and an appropriate model chosen. Many pastoral leaders have been trained in the counseling, therapeutic modality and are not as skilled in the experiental educational modality.

Planning Experientially for Family Growth Groups [1]

Experiential planning originates with the basic purpose for providing such experiences. This purpose is usually established by the sponsoring parish (or agency). In light of this purpose and other guidelines as found in chapter 4, a family enrichment model then would be chosen and the basic tenets of that model adopted; sometimes a compromise needs to be made between the congregation's purposes and the principles of the model. If a growth group model is adopted, a theoretical base is to use experiential education. (See chapter 4 about considerations in choosing a model.)

A "growth curriculum," from the human relations framework, is composed of the expressed needs of persons in the group and how these needs can be met through personal interactions, experiences, sharing, and outside input. In today's affluent society, the most neglected needs of middle-class people are those emotional ones which supply warmth, vibrancy, creativity, laughter, and spiritual "aliveness." These feelings can be either fostered or suppressed through the modeling of behavior, the reinforcement process, or group norms.

A growth curriculum for families deals with awareness of the total self, awareness of others within the family system, and awareness of how God is operative within family relationships. These learnings are achieved through the cluster interaction of one family and its individuals with other families and their individuals. Because each family system has its own way of interacting, the interpretation of these awarenesses differs among families.

From this consideration, a planning group would begin to collect information (called "data" in planning terms) from interested families. The planning group may be composed of the potential leaders, an interested group of people, or members of an educational committee. The data sought usually include:

1. How individuals perceive their family system,
2. The strengths and positive attributes of the family,
3. The deficiencies and negative attributes of the family,
4. Changes family members would like to see made,
5. Questions or concerns of individuals.

(A data collector used by a number of Family Cluster leaders is found in Appendix A.) The data collecting becomes the basic information from which curriculum is planned for a family growth group. By collating the data from family members, a profile of information about a family system can be identified; usually there is enough information in one set of data collectors to plan six months of cluster activities. They generate fantastic amounts of information! Generally, persons are fairly consistent with the way they actually behave in a real-life family setting and with information they've given on their data collectors. It appears that functioning family members have realistic perceptions of their family and are fairly open in exposing them. Often persons are pleased to know that their data giving was taken seriously in planning; the motivation and trust engendered by its use sometimes allow a group to delve deeper in topics untouched by the data-gathering instrument. Children in particular are delighted to know that their ideas and suggestions are taken seriously. This part of the process of experiential education becomes the motivator for further growth!

Also related to data is information about the leaders in terms of learned skills, innate abilities, personality characteristics, relationships they may have to individuals or families in the group, and expectations of themselves and of others. Other data would be considerations of space, equipment, times, and individual parish concerns.

When all the data is gathered, the leaders analyze and collate it around certain thematic areas which seem to be prevalent and consistent between individuals, between family members, and between family units. Data not usable at that time is often kept for further information at a later time. I find that I return to the data collectors for more information and insight after I've worked with families for two to three sessions. Experience has been in many family groups that lack of healthy communication, "put-downs," and the resolution of arguments ("hassling") seem to be topics common to a majority of families. Leaders decide on a beginning theme from general consensus about the information given and from what they know to be vital to healthy family functioning. There seems to be a homogeneity about family groups which makes such decisions relatively discernible.

Learning goals are then established for the thematic unit; this type of goal is described in several books listed in the Bibliography. Account is made of expectations and special interests, i.e., "I'm hoping for a lot of games," "I like to sing," "I think rhythmic movement is 'ugh'," "My father and I don't communicate," "I hope to make a lot of new friends." I have found that units usually work out to be six sessions in length, meaning six hours are given to consideration of one theme. This timetable may be modified by the number of sessions a group has, the interlude between group meetings, and length of time for each meeting. Experience has been that persons or families do not change after one or two exposures to a thematic idea because there are many variables in the learning/ change process. If a group meets once every seven days, it has many other input experiences from outside the group so that a new concept, a new skill, a new behavior takes time to germinate and to take root in living. Spread over four to six sessions, a unit of four to six hours' time will allow practice of some skills, time for discussion of meanings, evaluation, and closure. It also provides time for families to begin using the skills at home, with opportunity for questions and discussion between the cluster sessions.

Overall *goals* are set for a thematic unit which covers a sequence of time, say, six sessions. *Objectives* are set for each of the six specific sessions of that unit. For example, a thematic *goal* for a unit on communication might be "to introduce the concept of 'active listening' to families." A specific *objective* for one session in that unit may be, "By the end of this session, each family member will have taken turns being 'speaker,' 'listener,' and 'observer' within a simulated family in the cluster." Evaluation regarding the attainment of the objective can be checked at the conclusion of the session by asking:

1. Did each person in each family have a turn at all three positions (speaker, listener, and observer)?
2. Did each person assume all three positions?
3. What was not accomplished?
4. Who did not participate in all three roles?
5. Was anything else overlooked?

Session objectives are specific (they cover all facets), behavioral (they can be checked out by observation of behavior), measurable (they can be measured as to whether or not they were accomplished), and obtainable (they are able to be achieved in the session). A series of session objectives should be able to provide the participants with understanding and skills in achieving the overall goal. In a cluster session the leaders try to achieve a balance between cognitive input, actual skills practiced, and illustrations of individuals' experiences with the objective.

After setting goals for the unit, the leaders brainstorm by listing all the possible experiences which might be used with the group to accomplish those goals. Brainstorming means that an idea is offered, accepted, and listed on newsprint without comment or judgment. The advantage of having two leaders is apparent. Often one can turn to books to get further ideas or call someone who has had experience with that theme. Family members often provide assistance with brainstorming. Setting a time limit (usually ten minutes is enough) for the brainstorming activity seems to activate the thinking process and bring it to a reasonable conclusion.

At the conclusion of the time limit, brainstorming ideas are sorted in light of the specific objectives for the session and data on the individuals in the group; a tentative plan is developed for use with the specific group from which data was gathered. Sometimes the leaders need to return to the original information sheets to check out the use of a technique, family questions, or the number of persons wishing a certain topic to be used. The tentative plan includes:

- order of activities,
- assignment of tasks,
- length of time for each sector of the plan,
- transition possibilities,
- materials which need to be gathered or prepared,
- responsibility for setting up the learning environment for the group,
- areas to be practiced or worked on further.

Persons skilled with intergenerational group leadership have experiences from which they can draw regarding the interest of age groups, need for "change of pace" activities, developmental abilities, group mixing, etc. Inexperienced persons need to spend more time learning from actual experience regarding these areas. Coleaders who have worked together and are compatible can develop plans more quickly than persons new to each other. It is helpful to put all material on newsprint: collation of data by families, goal setting, brainstorming ideas, setting of objectives, and tentative session plans. These original "newsprint findings" are helpful later when the leaders evaluate the sessions. Sometimes a "dry run" or "walk-through" of the session plan, or part of the session, is helpful. This gives leaders an opportunity to

- have a "feel" for the activity,
- analyze its use with individuals in that specific group,
- see areas which need further clarifying,
- make a decision regarding the use of an activity,
- check on areas for which evaluation is wanted,
- raise further questions.

The greater the background of experience which leaders bring to a cluster situation, the more confidence they usually have to try new techniques and use new resources. On the other hand, a person new to leadership often adds a fresh perspective to the planning which a more experienced leader may never have tried or may have blocked from usage. It is helpful to set time limits on the planning, or these limits may be established by the leaders' time schedules. Before the session occurs, the leaders need to reflect together regarding the support they expect from each other; this provides security for them as they work with families.

When the learning environment has been set up, materials readied, and participants about to arrive, the leaders can relax and trust the process. They have done their best to be in readiness! I personally like to sit in the cluster room for a few minutes with a background of favorite music in order to be in preparation inside myself.

Designing for a family enrichment model is different from designing for other types of educational experiences. One needs to be aware of

- a multiplicity of experiences from which children, youth, and adults can find meaning,
- experiences which facilitate family interaction,
- unique needs of individuals and of families in the group,
- experiences which persons might find too threatening or confrontative in a family setting,
- experiences which have motivation for growth,
- experiences which attract the interests of various peer groups or subgroups within the cluster.

This blend, in terms of the unique factors in a cluster, makes planning for each cluster different and unlike any other.

Working Experientially in the Session

During a cluster session the experiential educator utilizes an action/reflection model which is known as "E-I-A-G-ing" in experiential terms. "E-I-A-G-ing" means the acts of *Experiencing—Identifying—Analyzing—Generalizing*. Adapting this process to a family cluster means:

1. Leaders guide members through *experiencing* a simulation in which all ages of cluster members usually can participate. This simulation experience is related to the theme of the unit, i.e., an exercise, a roleplay, the use of clay or finger paints, rhythmic movement, collage making, model building, fantasizing, or the like. Such techniques often are considered "child-centered" but are actually "experience-centered." If an experience is authentic, most people will respond and have feelings from that response which

become part of the learning situation. It is helpful for the leaders to move around the group in order to observe body behavior, to check who is speaking to whom, to watch for lack of response, to facilitate people to carry out the task comfortably, and to observe family interactions during the activity. Often experiences are instigated within simulated families composed of a father from one family, a mother from a second family, and children from third and fourth families. I like to compose simulated families ahead of time to facilitate the interaction of certain people who might not do so if random choosing were utilized. This method also takes care of the person who is always chosen last. Other groupings are dyads, triads, or quartettes, depending on the dynamics of the group and the behavioral objectives of the session.

2. The leaders lead the group members in quickly *identifying* their feelings and specific learnings from the simulation experience. Children will usually stay with the group during this period, as they have feelings about the experience to share. Often they provide tremendous insight to learnings that adults are afraid to admit or have blocked from their thinking. This is a point at which children can provide the models for risking and responding, as the sharing of feelings is not a "norm" of conventional behavior. Sometimes the leaders need to facilitate articulation by asking questions or helping persons distinguish between thoughts and feelings. They sometimes need to allow children to be heard if they are offering a valid contribution—or quiet children if they are divulging private family information. The leaders should provide assurance and safety for family units.

3. The leaders help the group in *analyzing* the exercise by asking what facilitated or blocked the process, how the persons were affected, and how the simulated exercise added to or disrupted their present learnings. When the group arrives at this point, the children will sometimes go to the play corner as a part of the group's contractual arrangement of allowing them to opt to leave an activity. This is the cognitive, analytical period of experiential learning when older children and adolescents contribute freely with adults. Many times this is when parents and other adults begin to have insights which they might wish to discuss at more length.

4. The leaders move the process to *generalizing* from learnings gained from the simulated experiences to persons' future behavior by using the questions, "What will you do differently another time?" "What new behaviors might be the outcomes of these learnings?"

"What do you want to try in your family now?" "What have you been doing well and how do you want to continue?" "What needs to be done differently in your family as a result of this experience?" "How might you contract around that area?" These questions provide an avenue for families to have new insights regarding change in their manner of operating. It can become a form of intentionalized learning which is a needed attribute for a world of rapid change. Often this is a point where the leader can interpret the children's insights into adult language. Sometimes a family unit becomes the "leader" for other family members through modeling, guiding discussion, raising questions, persuasion, or illustration. After the generalizing stage, sometimes it is helpful to have each family unit meet separately to discuss the next steps in an area of intent. Often the family ride home after the session becomes a time for further discussion of what has happened in the session. Thus, each family has the opportunity to relate and adapt the learnings to its own individual situation.

At times a cluster session "bombs"; such an incident can become a springboard for considering the session, the group's response, and the leadership behavior. Occasionally a group needs confronting about its behavior. Sometimes a leader needs to try, fail, and realize what he or she will *not* do again! I recall the first unit using transactional analysis I led; the children shared a great deal of negative evaluation about it. However, in the final evaluation for the program year, many of the children stated how they were using transactional analysis learnings in their various kinds of behaviors. Often learnings are internalized into behavior two to six weeks after they are introduced.

Evaluation becomes a springboard for planning the next session; leaders' observations are also helpful in planning. It has been the experience of many cluster leaders that a group can keep functioning at renewed levels through the use of experiential education. Through meeting needs of individuals and of families as they move through their developmental cycles, one can refocus on pertinent areas and not duplicate units. The group, through the process of growth, becomes able to renew itself. I led two family clusters for three program years, having a different coleader each six months. This led to a growth succession, and one cluster continued with other leaders for three additional years. The story of this "longest family group in cluster history" is told in *The Associate Reformed Presbyterian* magazine.[2] Intensive training experience in these processes will be described in the chapter on leadership.

Examples of Techniques for a Growth Curriculum

Suggestions for a growth curriculum start with the concept of the individual self, then enlarge to awareness of other selves. The family as a unit is also highlighted, plus the awareness of God's presence within family relationships. The cluster group, as a support community of care and affirmation, is also considered. The specific technique to be used at a certain time depends on the individual dynamics of the cluster. In light of the families within the cluster group, the leaders choose the specific techniques which they feel will best facilitate individuals within their family systems.

A curriculum for personhood (self) includes:

- affirmation of the person as a worthy human being;
- awareness of the facets of self: i.e., body, feelings, thoughts, perceptions, interpretations, intentions, actions, beliefs, assumptions, expectations;
- awareness of one's uniqueness;
- awareness of how one interacts and influences others;
- awareness of how one contributes to a human system of relationships within the family;
- awareness of how the family system contributes to one's self;
- awareness and delineation of inner strivings;
- encouragement and opportunity to express love for one's self.

Techniques which could contribute to such a curriculum are:

- drawing life-size silhouettes;
- adding to them comments of appreciation for that person;
- adding to them the person's attributes;
- writing or drawing notes of appreciation and affirmation;
- verbal sharing of appreciation and importance between persons;
- making appreciation gifts, i.e., "fuzzies," valentines;
- massaging, touching, hugging, stroking;
- celebrating "special times," i.e., birthdays, remembrances;
- singing or poetry reading about the "specialness" of persons.

A curriculum for developing awareness of others includes:

- contrasting the uniqueness of another person with self;
- presenting the uniqueness of another;
- understanding the importance of "tuning in" to another or empathizing;
- understanding how to communicate with others, which includes:

the process of self-disclosure,
the process of "checking out,"
the process of giving "straight" messages,
the process of receiving feedback,
the process of giving feedback,
the process of closure,

- affirming the other;
- receiving affirmation from others.

Techniques which could contribute to such a curriculum are:

- sharing the uniqueness of another;
- learning the many skills of communication, i.e., "active listening," receiving and giving both positive and negative feedback;
- role-playing the other's situation (reverse roles);
- "sculpting" a relationship and discussing it;
- drawing or forming faces from pieces of felt (or construction paper) as to feelings engendered in situations involving certain actions;
- modeling a structure together, i.e., using clay, Tinker Toys, pasteboard boxes, pipe cleaners, papier-mâché;
- working through conflicts with the use of bataccas (cloth hand bats), role play, sculpting;
- playing communication games;
- viewing a tape (video or cassette) of one's interactions;
- sharing affirmations via verbal, nonverbal, or written-means;
- using songs, poems, stories, quotations, posters, films, cartoons about communication and interactions;
- using puppets;
- using mime.

A curriculum for developing awareness of the family system, how one interacts within it, and how one is influenced by the system includes:

- understanding the uniqueness and contribution of each person to the system;
- understanding how the system works and what keeps it growing;
- noting and understanding the strengths, potentials;
- noting and understanding the weaknesses, blockages, hindrances for the system to operate successfully;
- assessing the value/belief of the system by what it actually does in behavior;

- affirming the system, as a totality, for what it is.

Techniques which could contribute to such a curriculum are:

- watching others role-play or sculpt in regard to their perceptions of one's family;
- receiving feedback from others;
- observing a videotape of one's family working on a task;
- using role reversal in role play;
- drawing or modeling the system, as it appears;
- receiving affirmation of the system through song, movement, cheer, ritual;
- sharing uniquenesses of the system;
- forming faces (via use of felt or construction paper) in response to certain situations within the system;
- contracting together;
- playing a game;
- puppet playing of various types of families, in contrast to each other;
- sharing in simulated families;
- working on a task together while under observation and receiving appropriate feedback;
- using songs, poems, stories, quotations, posters, pictures, cartoons, audiovisuals.

When growth is religious in quality, there is a feeling of identity and connectedness with a transcendent force larger than one's self or one's human system; yet it is still a part of one's person. In this force the person finds the furthest reaches of his or her aspirations, but the person realizes also—with poignancy—that these reaches will continuously stretch further beyond his grasp. Through becoming identified with this presence, the person feels a part of a universal community. For some people this presence is called "God," and its expression is called the "Holy Spirit." This intangible reality has been expressed through the ages by myths, stories, music, poetry, dance, art, rituals, and other symbolic forms. A curriculum for developing awareness of how God is operative within human relationships and systems includes:

- appreciating the love shown by God in the universe;
- understanding how God works through persons;
- developing awareness of ways persons can express love;
- realizing the interconnectedness of each human within the

system of the universe;

- understanding the ways each human hinders this interconnectedness from happening—or distorts it;
- appreciating modes in which persons have noted this reality through history, i.e., the Scriptures, liturgies, art forms, rituals;
- understanding and appreciating how other persons and cultures have expressed their interconnectedness with God.

Techniques which could contribute to such a curriculum are:

- considering the various facets of the "God reality" within human relationships, i.e., birth, growth, sexuality, death, afterlife;
- expressing feelings and reactions to these facets through the use of finger paint, clay, rhythmic movement, dance, free-flow drawing;
- ritualizing images together through the use of poems, chants, songs, prayers, movement, Scriptures, sacred writings, cheers, liturgies, symbols, instruments, rhythms;
- getting in touch with "the Spirit within" through the use of fantasizing, imaging, recalling and sharing dreams, praying, meditating, mythologizing, symbolizing, finger painting, listening to music;
- testifying (expressing appreciation) through words, songs, movement, creative writing, creative music and rhythm.

A human system needs a "community" which supports and nurtures it, thereby establishing "norms" to confirm persons' growing within their family system. Many groups and organized supports of the past have become meaningless to people today; so they need to compose their own support systems. Such a need is manifest with the emergence of many types of small groups, such as commune families, house churches, prayer groups, spiritual growth groups, encounter groups, intentional communities, and others. Family clusters are another form of support group for complete family units and emphasize the nurture and support of the family system within its cluster life. The curriculum for the cluster process includes:

- becoming aware and understanding how individuals and families influence other individuals and families;
- using ways which facilitate positive changes in the process of interaction;
- providing a "faith family" which can affirm, teach, support, and celebrate;

- providing a "people base" which fosters security, love, boundaries, and encouragement of its members;
- providing an opportunity for persons to make commitments from which they can grow.

Techniques which could contribute to such a curriculum are:

- contracting together;
- celebrating, worshiping, affirming;
- using group processes in decision making, problem solving, goal setting, evaluating to provide modeling for families;
- facilitating self and family disclosure;
- working on a common task together;
- having fun, enjoying each other;
- observing, sharing, discussing;
- using problems and "hurts" in facilitative ways to produce growth.

The components of a growth curriculum are expressed through human living by:

- persons who model ways of behaving in life situations;
- beliefs and values, as they are expressed through the modeling of persons and articulated with words;
- communication of those beliefs through body language, written expression, words;
- a "community" which centers around shared beliefs and sustains itself through certain behaviors, rituals, and expressions.

A "growth curriculum" needs "people expression." Growth is not the province of the professional/the educator/the minister/the leader/the teacher; rather it is the province of every person. An exciting happening in family enrichment is to observe the growth of each person, no matter what his or her age, within the family system and how it affects others. This growth process "snowballs" within the family setting and ". . . these approaches seek to liberate directly an entire relationship system—so that everyone in that network will be freer to grow."[3]

Resources

You, as a person, are the most important resource you bring to a family growth group. One's presence in authentic living with others becomes the context for healthy, interpersonal resources. One's ability to synthesize elements from various theories of learning becomes the keyboard for choosing learning experiences wisely. One's modeling becomes the visible personhood from which others can develop. The person/leader is like an orchestra conductor who cues in one section of instruments (one family), then a combination of instruments (groups of persons), and finally the full orchestra (the whole cluster group) through a combination of rhythms and notes.

The individuals in the cluster are resources inasmuch as they contribute ideas, abilities, interactions, creative abilities, their own self-disclosure, and behaviors. Many individuals and families are not used to contributing to the learning process; so they need encouragement and opportunity. The family units are resources which contribute modeling, family-disclosure, and interactions. These units are the foundation stones of the cluster. The worth of items used, such as books, audiovisuals, songs, etc., can only be measured in how the meanings within them are expressed by persons' behavior.

Since there is no single manual or leader's book to use in family growth groups, a number of helpful books and resources are suggested in the Bibliography. Those which I find usable for many situations are starred with an asterisk. Book resources fall into several categories:

1. Those which have exercises for use in thematic areas;
2. Those which tell about the use of techniques with various age groups;
3. Those which present information to use in cluster, i.e., stories, poems, songs, prayers, readings, games;
4. Those which present background information on thematic material so leaders can be aware of concepts, knowledge, and research in certain fields;
5. Those which interpret leadership skills and knowledge for leading family groups.

One of the most versatile books is Virginia Satir's *Peoplemaking*.[4] In it she tells about the importance and influence of the family system and presents exercises related to the areas of self-worth, communication, power, and rules. Many new books are being produced in related fields, and it is helpful to be aware of advertisements and book reviews. The public library is a valuable resource and often will order new books and records which are helpful to leaders. A church library might devote part of its budget to family leadership materials helpful both to leaders and family members. A resource listing of books, films, stories, records, and other items which a group of family cluster leaders often have used is available from Family Clustering, Inc.[5] Family Clustering also publishes a quarterly newsletter, *The Purple Turtle,* which describes many resources and techniques used by cluster leaders around the country.[6]

I keep file folders on each theme I've used in a cluster or those themes I hope to develop. As I find any material related to a specific theme, such as books, cartoons, pictures, films, cassettes, information, songs, posters, and the like, I put it in the folder for keeping. When I need to brainstorm about a certain theme which a cluster has requested, I have a file folder of ideas. Some thematic areas used in clusters are:

> communication—family histories—rituals—beliefs and values— the future of the family—interpersonal relations—sexuality— death and dying—conflict resolution—creative problem solving— decision making—family destiny—family strengths—poverty— ecology—world hunger—freedom and responsibility—dreams and hopes—power and its expression—transactional analysis— family systems—careers and vocations—self-worth—"becoming" as persons and families—fantasies—prayer and meditation—and others.

Other types of resources I've found helpful to have on hand are catalogs of posters, films, filmstrips, cassettes, records, places of interest, games, ideas from other clusters, etc. Many of these are free, and I find it valuable to be on a number of mailing lists. The exchange of mimeographed idea sheets and condensed items with others brings new material to one's leadership file. A group of cluster leaders may want to meet periodically and share resources with each other.

The use of records, cassettes, and tapes can be contributed by teenagers; many of the popular songs have meaningful words which can be springboards for further discussion. I keep some records for group singing, dancing, rhythmic movement, background listening, painting, or learning songs. Guitars, autoharps, banjos, harmonicas, recorders, and rhythm instruments all add to enjoyment of music. Popular games and stunts are fun and can be found in Scout manuals, 4-H resources, libraries, and books for use in Y programs.

The supply type of resource is simple and easily obtained; many items can be found in supply rooms of church schools, nursery schools, public schools, scouting groups. Useful items are.

large newsprint (some people use old newspapers with fluorescent markers), marking pens in assorted colors (water-based colors are easily washed out of clothing), masking tape, any kind of magazine or catalog for cutting, glue, crayons, pipe cleaners, felt scraps, clay or play-dough, finger paint and paper, construction paper, Styrofoam containers and packing, egg cartons, pieces of cloth, yarn, rickrack, and sewing odds and ends, buttons and sequins, artificial flowers, Popsicle sticks, cardboard boxes.

A budget of approximately one hundred dollars per year will keep several clusters supplied for a twenty-five-week period. Since there is no expensive curriculum to purchase nor extensive equipment needed, the budgeted amount is usually adequate. Some churches charge families a nominal fee for the use of supplies.

Useful Techniques

Since our society is a didactic one, it is commonly thought that verbalizations are the more sophisticated tool of learning. Our schools of higher education reflect this belief, and it becomes "counter-cultural" to try other techniques. The presence of children in a learning group provides a legitimate excuse to try other techniques; as they learn with the action/reflection mode, persons realize the value of these techniques for further learnings. Such is particularly true when one works with feelings and emotional interactions which need to be expressed in behaviors. The leaders must believe in the techniques and feel comfortable in their introduction. It is helpful to catch the children's interest and enthusiasm so they can model the use of a new technique enthusiastically; this often propels a group into using it! As adolescents and adults begin to get into the swing of a new technique, this can become a tool for experiencing feelings which are difficult to articulate or are just below the surface of consciousness. These feelings become visible evidence of a new world in the person and also become data which leaders can use in future sessions for further understanding of an individual or family, as well as to promote new growth directions.

If a newly discovered feeling or learning is too painful for a person, often he or she will not disclose it through usual ways in the group. Sometimes it may be cloaked in humor, and often the adolescents are the first to see through it! Usually such feelings are accompanied by nonverbal expressions of anxiety, embarrassment, and tension: high-pitched laughter, red faces, squeaky voices, restlessness, etc. A leader needs to be aware of what subjects and actions embarrass a participant and how this embarrassment is expressed nonverbally. Virginia Satir feels that no subject in family living can be taboo if healthy thinking about all facets of life is to be facilitated. Many families have not dealt openly with taboo subjects in front of children or adolescents. Sometimes an adult hears natural articulation about a "closed" subject for the first time when it is aired without being smothered by fear and embarrassment. A well-timed song, rhyme, chant, or pun may ease tension.

Techniques which can be used with all age groups to get at feelings and hidden concepts are:

finger painting, clay modeling, role playing, family sculpting, creative writing, rhythmic movement, drawing and painting, model building from all types of three-dimensional sculpting materials, collage making, song making, scrapbook making, completing reactions to pictures, completing metaphors, completing fill-in statements, responding to songs, rhythms, music, seeing films and filmstrips, learning new songs, hearing stories, poems, and prayers, ritual making, interviewing, fantasizing, "dreaming," using simulation games, observing "fish bowl" style, and numerous others.

Since family dynamics are not expressed openly in groups within our culture, the leaders need to be sensitive to appropriate and inappropriate responses from individuals and families. Sometimes the exposed pain of a family dynamic is a relief, and families often are open to new realization after the blocking pain is exposed. Sometimes the freedom is needed to "opt out" of experiences in some sessions, so as to convince a highly educated father, an uptight mother, or a reticent adolescent that it is OK to take time to become familiar with a new process of learning. If the contractual item of individual choice regarding participation is followed, usually a leader can introduce a different technique or a new way of expression. Sometimes the joyful, spontaneous ego state of children and some adults will provide the opening for an unusual approach. Often I've introduced a new technique as a "fun experience" to give persons an opportunity to "feel" into finger painting, rhythmic movement, or creative writing. Their own success is further momentum for experiencing.

The following criteria are helpful in the consideration of a technique and its application to an idea:

1. Does it "speak" to the child's experience? Can the child draw ideas and concepts from the material with which she or he is familiar?
2. Does it avoid excessive symbolism?
3. Is there some motion or physical movement to the activity?
4. Does the content offer family members an opportunity to reinforce each other as individuals?
5. Does it provide validity for growth in religious response?
6. Is the leader unafraid to accept the group's responses?

There are many books which explain preparation for use of a technique, directions to give, and adaptations to make. Most libraries have books related to crafts and creative expression. Many books on preschool education explain ways these activities can be used with young children. Often leaders in 4-H, Scouts, preschools, Y groups, and clubs are familiar with creative activities and sponsor workshops which teach people how to use them.

Ritualizing is sometimes an unfamilar technique in groups within our society. A ritual is a prescribed form, known by all participating, for the performance of a rite or ceremony. It usually involves acknowledgment of the intangible realities between human beings, such as love, trust, faith, and goodness. Churches and other institutions of religious faith have been the leading perpetuators of rituals. Their use is important to group cohesion, and they contribute to the strength of family life.[7] Many persons no longer find meaning in the traditional forms of religious ritual; therefore, clusters encourage persons to make their own rituals. When a ritual evolves from the life of a group, it holds rich meaning for all in that group. Areas around which family clusters may develop rituals are:

grace before meals, cluster "council," closure and farewell, holidays, celebrations for special events, resolution of conflict, affirmation of individuals and families.

The Family Group Room

A group's "space" is like a home; it can represent security for persons and provide a warm, hospitable setting to which people will want to come. A feeling of warmth and security is of great importance to a family group. Most church educational buildings are fashioned after schools, with sterility and conformity. A "rule of thumb" for the room in which a family group meets is to make it as much like a home living space (for thirty people) as possible. A large "lounge-like" space with a carpet is best for the informal atmosphere of the group. The room should be wide enough to make a comfortable circle and large enough for families to be separated when they are working individually. A fireplace is a wonderful asset! Comfortable furniture, such as couches, chairs, and lamps, suggest "belongingness." People can sit on the rug or on chairs. Rug sitting allows children to be at the same level as adults and also makes for informality and fun. Many large halls can be made smaller and more cozy with the use of room dividers, heavy blankets, mattresses, rugs, and cushions.

A play/toy corner is important for children, as it suggests that their needs are considered; it also provides an alternative place for free expression when children opt to leave an activity. The most appreciated toys are those which can be built together to provide for new experiences, such as Tinker Toys, Lego blocks, building blocks, trains, small play cars, etc. Giant Tinker Toys are excellent. Large-wheeled toys, such as are found in nursery schools, are fun. Rules for the use of the play corner should be included in the contract of the cluster. Usually young children are cooperative when they are a part of intergenerational contracting and when their ideas are taken seriously.

If a group has a large number of young children and babies, a safety corner with playpens and adequate equipment might need to be established. Special times might be reserved for the more noisy toys in order to keep some semblance of order when families are involved in activities. Sometimes when younger children are involved in the play corner while their families are working on an activity, one of the leaders can be discussing and sharing the same topic with the younger children. Often used is the teaching media of puppets and songs around the same topic the others are considering. Most parents and preschool teachers know how to facilitate freedom and safety for young children in a play group. If creative equipment is available, often older children will join in a play corner and provide modeling in play with the younger ones.

Older children enjoy access to a supply shelf where materials provide opportunity for free expression, so feelings can be dealt with and expressed constructively. Materials to use are scrap paper, clay, crayons, markers, catalogs, pipe cleaners, cloth, cardboard, Styrofoam, etc. Many times older children and preschoolers will begin to play together, and this intergenerational "mix" provides another learning experience for the children who are involved.

A few cupboards, shelves, or tables for storage of supplies are helpful. A record player is an asset which can be used in many ways. It is helpful to have open wall spaces to hang newsprint directions, quotes, pictures, posters, and items that have been constructed by the group. Young children take great delight in hanging their work on the wall and having it acknowledged. I often use a child's song, poem, art work, or puzzle creation as a way to have the group consider the force of creative activity. Sometimes this freedom provides the opportunity for creative work by adults.

If the group has meals together, space for setting up tables and chairs is needed, or they may be set up in another room. The closeness of water and a kitchen aids in meal preparations.

Some groups utilize private homes for their meeting place, which can present some unique problems. In her home setting the hostess usually controls the timing and spacing of the group, so less time is available for the structured learning parts of the program. Sometimes it is difficult to hang materials on the walls and to use "messy" techniques. Special attention needs to be given to the shared use of children's playthings, since most middle-class children "own" their toys. Home settings are excellent places in which to have occasional parties and celebrations; this provides a different environment from the regular cluster room. In southern climes, groups meet on outdoor patios or in a picnic spot. Every cluster can enjoy a hike, a parade, a picnic, or a retreat setting for a change of pace. Using the "neutrality" of a church's space has advantages—it is not private for part of the group; its use is more free from hidden expectations; and everyone starts with the same sense of ownership. If a church is sponsoring an enrichment group, providing tangible space is one symbol of its sponsorship and belief in the group.

Budgeting and Fee Structures

When a church or agency sponsors family enrichment as a part of its regular program, it is usually financed through the total budget. This assures that time and energy have been exerted to "sell" a different philosophy and program to the ongoing committee which determines budget. If an organization uses staff members or volunteers as leaders, the leadership fee is inherent in their salaries or volunteer contributions. If a church hires an outside skilled leader, budget will need to be allocated for this leadership. A well-trained cluster leader can train another person through the apprenticeship mode; thus an organization would be receiving leadership services as well as training opportunities for its one fee. Family Clustering, Inc. can serve as a liaison between qualified persons and organizations intent on providing these services.

Sometimes families are requested to contribute a set fee toward family enrichment, particularly if they do not have membership in the sponsoring agency. Since churches have little experience in fee-paying structures, they sometimes hesitate to charge a fee. Family enrichment might be likened to a preventive health activity or family recreation; a fee for twelve sessions might be equivalent to the amount a family would pay for one dinner at a moderately priced restaurant.

It has been suggested that health insurance companies consider deductions from a family premium if the family seriously undertakes preventive education because of its relation to the prevention of emotional and psychiatric disorders. The Aid Association for Lutherans in Wisconsin gives deductions to parents who participate in the Parent Effectiveness Program through their parochial schools because of their belief that good parent education is prevention against emotional debilitation. An agency which claims to value improving the quality of the human condition might consider expressing this philosophy in financial terms.

The following quote seems appropriate in summarizing the effects of a "growth curriculum" and its expressive resources: "Much more than the use of gimmicks and techniques, success seems geared to how effectively the group is able to respond to its very human needs in a manner that exploits no one and maximizes its own potential."[8]

CHAPTER 6

Leadership in a Family Enrichment Group

Most of us can tell what positions are ones of leadership or point out which persons are the leaders in a group; however, to define the concept of leadership is a more difficult task. Findings from research seem to indicate that leaders do not possess specific qualities which demarcate them from nonleaders. Who will become a leader "depends upon a complex of forces which do not permit prediction." [1] A person may be a leader by position, through situations, or by functions which need to be performed. Leadership may be defined as "the performance of those acts which help the group achieve its goals." [2]

In our culture it is necessary for families to assume leadership to fulfill the tasks needed for their own interpersonal functioning. When families join a cluster, automatically there are several family subgroups with their own leadership patterns and ways of assigning leadership for their family units. Added to this, there is the emotional interaction between parents and children with inbuilt facets of responsibility and loyalty. This makes for a complexity of factors in terms of leadership within a family enrichment group.

Basically "leadership is . . . the execution of a particular kind of role within an organized group, and [essentially] this role is defined . . . in terms of power or the ability to influence others." [3] Power is a complex force, particularly so within a family group, because it has so much potency within family dynamics. This strength can be used for growth and fulfillment or for destruction and devastation. Virginia Satir states that the main forces of power in the family can be defined by these adjectives: vigorous, forceful, strong, influential, energetic, controlling, regulating, restraining, and curbing.[4] Power is essential to every human being; often patterns of power in a family emerge from those patterns which the adults learned as children within their own families.[5] Many times a group is faced with two family members involved in a power conflict which brings to the surface numerous subconscious reactions from others in the group. It also activates energy in persons occupying similar roles in other families. For instance, if a mother and son in a family are locked in a "power play" within their own dynamics, this situation can arouse feelings in other mother-son relationships among the adult males in the group (who were sons), the adult females in the group (who have sons), and the younger males in the group (who are sons). A chain reaction of this kind happens instantaneously! It also activates energy among the mother figures in the families, the sons, and others who move in to form coalitions with mothers or sons. In many respects, power within family groups presents more complexity to leadership than in peer-oriented groups.

Whether or not leadership is designated in a family group, there will always be the emergence of some persons who will assume power over others and over the group. Unless a group is aware of this force, usually a "control issue" will emerge, and the group will remain locked in power struggles. They will wonder why they "don't seem to be getting anywhere." This issue saps energy and consumes time of the individuals involved; so their opportunity for growth is curtailed. I recall one cluster in a laboratory where a peer group of three young boys controlled the cluster and had everyone unsettled in the group— the leaders, the parents, the other children, and the adults in training. The cluster could not function in a growth style because of the diverted energy used by these boys to keep the group going "in circles." The intervention of an outside consultant was used to observe, to diagnose the situation, and to rechannel the power energy of these three boys into constructive behavioral outlets. After that intervention, the cluster was able to move in growth patterns because the power of these three boys had been channeled from blocking activity to creative use through having their basic needs met. Usually a cluster group is so involved in its own dynamics that it is not aware of these forces at work; therefore an outside consultant is helpful in providing an objective observation of just what is happening in the group so that a diagnosis can be made and steps taken to resolve the problem.

Leadership in a Family Enrichment Group

In the case of a family growth group, there is a complexity of factors out of which leadership emanates:

- the leader of each family;
- the perceived leader in certain situations in a family;
- the assigned leaders of the group;
- the leaders of subgroups which may emerge, i.e., the teenagers;
- a family unit which assumes leadership as a unit within a cluster activity;
- individuals who emerge at times as "leader figures" through designation or by their own activity.

This section will deal primarily with the designated leadership styles, as listed in the various enrichment models in a previous chapter. The leadership style of any particular model is due to the history of the model, the understanding of power and leadership within family systems, and the beliefs about leadership within the assumption base of the model. The types of leadership in family enrichment modes may be considered in these ways:

1. *Rotating leadership*
   among various individuals in the group
   among various family units in the group
2. *Assigned leadership*
   to an individual, chosen by the group's participants
   to a family unit, chosen by the group's participants
   to an individual, chosen by the sponsoring organization,
       i.e., the church, synagogue, agency
3. *No assigned leadership*

Rotating Leadership

One advantage of rotating leadership is that no one person or family unit needs to spend a lot of time in leadership planning and tasks; the responsibility is shared among all persons in the group. Each family, or person, has an opportunity to present an interest, and many times the act of planning becomes a family activity itself. The opportunity for personal dynamics to build and to become activated in response to one leader becomes nil; the group is not stuck with one person in that responsibility.

Some of the inherent disadvantages of rotating leadership are that a family group does not stay with one topic long enough to have it influence the behavior of the families; the growth aspect is limited because change is not nurtured and developed after the seed of an idea is first planted. In Family Clusters our experience has been that six to eight sessions are needed for a common set of ideas to be learned and to be internalized into family systems, so that change can be experienced. With rotated leadership, group members need to adjust to a different authority style each session and to spend their energy deciding what they can do or cannot do in a given situation; this is particularly true of children. With the rotating style of leadership, often it occurs that the group chooses to meet in the home of a different leader each week, providing the additional dimension of becoming acquainted with each family's private home. Not only does the leader have group responsibility but also the responsibility of hostessing, decision making about children's play, utilizing space, etc. It might be wise for a group with rotating leadership to meet in a home other than the leader's in order to avoid heavy responsibility on the part of one person.

Assigned Leadership
. . . by the group

An advantage of group assignment of leadership is that the participants can determine whom they want for a leader, thereby maintaining control over the group's functions and programs. Usually the person, or family, chosen is homogenous with the others and is likely to have more understanding of the group's concerns. Probably the participants will have some understanding of the manner in which the leader will operate and will know what to expect from that person. If the chosen leader has skills in group leadership and in family relations, these can be used as a model for other families through the techniques of "fish-bowling," "active listening," problem solving of real issues which arise. This modeling presents an authentic situation from which families can observe and learn.

Sometimes there are adolescents in the group who have leadership skills and the desire to express them; they serve as a helpful "third person" on a leadership team through finding challenge but not having full responsibility. Usually it is difficult for an adolescent to be a major leader to adults, particularly when some of those adults are one's parents!

Diametrically opposite, an individual serving as leader with his or her own family in the group is sometimes caught in a number of restraints:

- choosing to be in one's family role over that of the leadership role;
- choosing between one's own members and another family's members for an activity;
- being considered biased *against* one's family members;
- being considered biased *for* one's family over other families;
- having one's family take out its frustration about leadership at another time in another setting.

With the presence of one's family in the group, a leader has extra concerns of which to be aware:

- how to cope with intense personal feelings related to family members;
- how to cope with family members' feelings;
- how to cope with feelings engendered by the leadership roles;
- how to cope with feelings and actions of the coleader;
- how to cope with the total group reactions;
- how to facilitate the group in such a situation.

With this type of leadership, a group would find it helpful to use an outside consultant when it strikes a blockage, as the leader/parent cannot be expected to stand back and to see the problem from all sides. To add to the concern, young children will often "act out" the feeling tone of the parent/leader and embarrass the parent before the group. The parent/leader is then faced with the dilemma of how to handle the child in front of the group. In one cluster the parent/leader insisted on having his family in the group. By the third session, interaction had escalated to the point that the parent/leader had to tell his family to leave the cluster because of the inconsistency created. The difficulty emerged between the discipline of his children and expectations of the leadership role. Such an event becomes the emotional agenda for the group, though it may not be verbalized; the energy and time of the group is absorbed by this concern. Experience and observation of many groups show that few leaders can handle gracefully the dynamics of the presence of their own family!

When a family unit, as a whole, assumes the leadership role, it is difficult to get the whole family together to plan. Often planning is assumed by one person in the family, usually the mother; she wants her family to perform its task but has a begrudged feeling of being saddled with the responsibility which belongs to the whole family. If the older children or adolescents have not been involved in the decision to be the leadership family, they may use this incident to express rebellion against decisions made for them. The time for program planning is spent, then, in hassling and arguing. If leadership directions are decided by the adults only in a family group, norms about the unimportance of children in decision making become established, which are difficult to retract. This also sets the precedent that children are not as important as adults in the power sector of decision making.

. . . by the sponsoring organization

When a church or organization sponsors family enrichment, it may choose the leaders. If the sponsor recruits the leaders, it will be responsible for their morale and group work. An advantage of this type of assigned leadership is that the organization supports the concept and the program. It may do this by screening leaders, by providing training, and by budgeting money resources. If persons have confidence in the organization, this provides a security base out of which to try new models of education. Persons' confidence in the leadership is often reflective of their confidence in the sponsoring agency.

Some disadvantages with this form of leadership are: the leader is assigned, and the participants have no choice of leader; if a leader behaves inappropriately, the group may disintegrate rather than follow the problem back to the source; such may be particularly true with a volunteer leader. This in turn will disrupt the church's purpose for having enrichment activities and deadlock the potential for change.

No Assigned Leadership

A group which has no designated form of leadership may function well with a convener who undertakes the administrative tasks of the group. Since this type of group often is established for fun and fellowship, the need for programming is not important for group maintenance. If the group decides occasionally on a type of programming, the leadership may be recruited from within the group. In the Extended Family Model of Unitarian-Universalist churches, often members are persons from the upper-middle class with educational, creative, and financial resources which make it easier to utilize this type of model. My experience with Extended Family groups has been that they want more depth and sharing after a year or so of socializing; therefore, their reason for having family enrichment changes. As a result, there is a need to reconsider the kind of enrichment wanted and to recontract relative to the new intentions.

One advantage of this leadership form is that no one needs to assume the responsibility for leadership. A disadvantage is that a group may often "spin its wheels" in discussing what to do and have little energy left to do something after a decision is made. If a person appears to be assuming leadership in group facilitation, the person may be criticized for assuming a role which the group did not bestow.

Criteria for Choosing a Type of Leadership

Questions may be asked from which criteria can be developed to help churches determine the type of leadership needed for family enrichment. Some of these questions are:

1. What is the *reason* a family enrichment group is started?
   - Is it sponsored by a "parent organization" or by an individual for a reason inherent in the organization's philosophy?
   - Is it an ad hoc group which meets because of its own interests and values?
   - Is it a service offered to families by an agency?
   - Is it a service offered to families by an individual who makes money from the service?
   - Is it a selection of unrelated families who are attempting to meet some of their needs?
2. What is the *purpose* of the family enrichment group?
   - Is it to teach prescribed structured material to families, i.e., theological or religious content, communication skills, relationship skills?
   - Is it to facilitate families, through a growth group, to deal with their own concerns, dreams, questions, problems, hopes?
   - Is it to encourage families to have fun and enjoyment?
   - Is it to encourage intentional growth directions within a specific family system, as determined by an expert?
3. What *leadership* is available?
   - Does an agency or church have the needed leadership within its own organization?
   - Does a church need to provide financial and support resources to obtain skills and formation to train its own leadership?
   - Does a church or agency need to hire an outside leader?

- Does a group need to consider the possibility of cooperating with other organizations to obtain leadership?
- Does an organization believe in the purpose enough to plan and work to obtain leadership?

Motivating and Recruiting Leaders

Motivating persons to become leaders of family enrichment is much like motivating them for any other leadership capacity within a volunteer organization. Motivation is aroused because of a felt need, a desire to learn in new areas, and a sense of fulfillment. Persons with well-functioning families are good ones to be approached; often such persons are using good parenting skills and healthy ways of interacting. They may be representative of varied age groups: i.e., young adults who are beginning their family living and are aware of its potential, because of the well functioning in their "family of origin." Also to be considered are middle-aged adults who are looking for some new outlets of leadership at the same time their children are beginning to become independent. Older adults whose children are grown and who are aware of the influence the family exerts on persons make helpful leaders. Not to be overlooked are single persons who want family ties through facilitating family groups. Often more women will volunteer than men, as culturally, women sense the need for family education because of their proximity to the nurturing, growing process. As it becomes more acceptable for men to be interested in the process of family nurturing, they may volunteer in greater numbers. Some persons may have ceased accepting responsibilities for the usual kinds of church teaching positions but would like other leadership opportunities. Participation in a family enrichment event is one way to motivate people to see the potentialities of this form of education by experiencing it with their own family. In Family Cluster leadership, the definite time period encouraged by the contracting process gives persons a leadership opportunity within set time limits. The training process provides useful skills and information for their own family living when leadership is finished.

Screening is important for leadership recruitment in any church venture because of the nature of volunteerism. The recruitment process might encompass:

- observing people living in their family situation;
- seeking persons who would like to give time and energy to

facilitate family living;
- assuring persons that training and support would be offered;
- placing persons in an apprenticeship situation with a skilled leader;
- providing consultant services to leaders as individuals, as group leaders, and as family members;
- supporting the leaders with morale, budget, encouragement, and recognition.

A parish needs to provide volunteers with these assets because of the nature of the task and gravity of the purpose.

Often cluster leaders want an enrichment experience for their families; sometimes this can be experienced by having the family be members of another cluster; or this could be provided through ecumenical interchange or sponsorship of an enrichment event for leaders' families. I discovered an excellent way to obtain feedback on my cluster leadership was to have another leader and her family in a cluster I led. A church may be able to schedule clusters so a person can lead for a term (twelve sessions) and then the leader's family can be members in a different cluster another term (twelve weeks).

Persons, by serving in an apprenticeship position, are more able to assess their readiness and potential for leadership. Often graduate students serve well as coleaders while implementing their cognitive learning with practical experience. Many colleges and universities offer credit toward course requirements in the fields of pastoral counseling, religious education, social work, family studies, mental health, and other courses in the helping professions. Frequently students are highly motivated and able to use assignment time for planning. They may bring a fresh approach to leading which is an asset with adolescents and children in a cluster. The experience also provides a setting in which young adults can learn firsthand about family systems and how to effect change in them, an invaluable learning for their own family and professional lives.

Recruitment of leadership can be conducted beyond one's own church or organization. Many social work agencies are becoming interested in the prevention of family crises and wish to learn experiential educational techniques; moreover, persons from these agencies may offer a valuable understanding of family systems. Some communities have used an ecumenical approach in clustering where a leader from one church coleads in another church to help clusters get started, and the second coleader reciprocates. Ecumenical interfaith clusters provide one of the best ways for cross-fertilization of values and beliefs. I observed recently in a cluster sponsored by a "liberal" church in which there was a family from a very authoritative church system. During the contracting, a parent was confronted regarding the expressed inconsistency between the behavior of children and the scriptural stance which had been used. Later the parent stated a desire to change toward more congruency and asked the group to give feedback in regard to behavior. Such an interchange helps people to consider their value system with its behavioral component and helps children to observe different ways of believing and behaving. This is an important learning for living in a pluralistic world.

Some persons state that they feel family enrichment demands professional leadership or knowledge gained in a degree program. I have worked with many lay volunteers in leadership roles and feel they can be as effective as professional leaders in the facilitating of families when they learn certain skills. In regard to training for those in the helping professions, Robert Carkhuff states:

> Lay counselors [facilitators] can effect significant constructive change in clients. One implication, then, is that the process of one individual attempting to help another is not the exclusive province of professional helpers.[6]

Personality Characteristics of a Facilitating Leader

An emotionally healthy person, from a mental health perspective, is the most important leadership ingredient for a growth group of families. One cannot train a leader to be a healthy, functioning individual; this is a "given" with which the person comes to the leadership role. Some of the characteristics of a facilitating leader are:

- insight into personal needs and how some of these are met in the leadership role;
- willingness to work on interpersonal relations;
- willingness to share one's personal pilgrimage;
- warmth and caring;
- awareness of one's own value system while maintaining respect for the value system of others;
- ability to deal with all generations at once in an open process;
- ability to communicate understandings and insights to several age groups at once;
- time and motivation for preparation;
- willingness to grow and to change;
- openness to differences and the process of coping with them.

A healthily functioning person is a growing person, reaching out for other growth opportunities; so the productive energy of the Creator is channeled through the relationships the person has with others. Such a person cultivates and uses techniques which facilitate keeping in touch with this Spirit—meditation, prayer, yoga, reading from the writings of others who have been on pilgrimage, worship, Bible study, creative activities, etc.

In a family growth group, such as the Family Cluster, two leaders are recommended since so many dynamics exist in a cluster system of four or five family subsystems. Therefore, a leader needs to be able to work in a team relationship with all of its dynamics. A male/female team is usually most helpful for both males and females in the group. Leadership teams can be composed of husbands and wives or any persons who care about each other. If a husband/wife team is in leadership, they need to be aware of their own dynamics and how that influences the group; their positive modeling, as a couple, will provide strong potential for facilitating marriage/family relationships for the group. If they have children, they may wish to decide whether or not the group will benefit from the dynamics of the presence of their children. It may be that children will take too much time and energy from the group because of reasons listed earlier. Most children find it difficult to share both parents in a leadership role. The couple will also need more time for planning; often their own relationship will need attention before group planning will be productive. Planning always follows relationship building.

In many instances a female/male team, composed of two individuals not married to each other, can model understanding, care, and affection for each other. This provides an opportunity for families to observe that affection and caring need not only be shared among family members but also can be a vital part of a human community. Any team needs to work on its own relationship before designing a cluster session. Often two persons can complement each other in personality and leadership style so there are more facets of growth being offered to a group composed of multi-generations and family subgroups. Some people may be fearful of sexual intimacies between leaders; the more open two leaders are about their relationship and how this affects their leadership roles, the more honesty is shown before the group. Leaders need to be mature individuals who know how to handle their sexual feelings and intimacies appropriately in family group settings. Sex is a taboo subject in our culture, particularly when children are present. My experience has demonstrated that greater sensitivities are needed in a family group than in a peer group when discussing this subject. Often such awareness is sensitized in the leader by attending sexuality workshops where one can become more conscious of his or her own sexuality and how it may be expressed in creative, healthy ways.

Sexuality is one of the most potent areas of life, but it has been presented in distorted fashion in much of our culture; so there is a need to be realistic yet prudent. Such awareness is reiterated sometimes when a cluster includes a single woman who may reach out to men in the group for friendship, or a male adolescent may be attracted to an adult female in the group. Sexuality, with such individualistic expression, must be dealt with in an individual manner with the persons involved; usually the leaders need to utilize their awareness and skills in bringing such an issue to the surface to be discussed. We have had two leaders of the same sex often lead a family cluster and work well together. The same needs for interpersonal relating and leading are evident here. Coleaders bring a greater number of ideas and resources to the planning and refining process, possess a wider range of perceptions, and are able to observe the group more closely.

Skills Important to Family Cluster Leadership

The remainder of the chapter will deal explicitly with leadership of the Family Cluster Model, which is a growth group for family systems. Many of the same skills are important for other family enrichment models but are not as crucial because those models do not depend on group processes. The Family Cluster utilizes the leadership style of a facilitator; in that role the leaders help a group to get started, to share power among all participants through contracting, and to aid the family members in determining what the group agenda will be. The leaders do not bring a ready-made agenda to the group but help the group determine its own agenda out of their family concerns, questions, problems, dreams, hopes, and joys. A leader serves in a many-faceted role, using different leadership styles in accordance with what seems appropriate to group needs, family needs, and individual needs. These needs are blended during a session; and the skill a leader develops, through experience, is to know *when* what style is needed and *how* to behave with that style. This suggests that a leader become eclectic in his or her own unique way of operating. Robert Carkhuff suggests:

... the most effective helpers need no system [or therapy]; they draw upon all systems and create their own to meet the very unique and individualized programs that will enable helpers to function effectively.[7]

A basic skill needed in a growth model is the understanding and facilitating of interpersonal processes between all ages of human beings, including communication skills, conflict resolution skills, decision-making skills, relating skills, etc. The more experience a leader has in using these skills with various age groups, the more easily such attributes will be utilized by families in their ongoing process of living together through putting to work their learnings at home. Carkhuff sees the interpersonal process at the heart of all helping processes. The basic behavior of healthy relating works at all age levels, but conceptual and technique modifications can be utilized to help children and youth sense a leader is attuned to them—listening to the children and youth during group time and accepting their contributions. Being accepted and listened to is not a typical cultural experience for children meeting with adults, and children are very quick to perceive when they have the attention of an adult.

Another leadership understanding is how family systems work and are organized. Each family has its own unique way of operating, and one needs to be aware of dysfunctioning systems as well as healthy ones. Often one facet of the family system is dysfunctioning, but the other facets function well enough to keep the family system from searching for outside help. The family is "hurting" in one aspect, and a leader can sometimes sort out the problem or "hurt" and attend to its healing with the resources people bring to the group.

A leader needs to be acceptant of all types of families, particularly of those whose value systems and manner may differ from one's own. This is particularly true when working with families from a different socioeconomic level or an ethnic, cultural context. Families from every sector have strengths, and a leader can be cognizant of these when acceptance of differences is recognized. Since the Family Cluster Model is *not* a therapy model, it is important to know when it might be appropriate to intervene, as an educator, in the family and when it might not be appropriate. Also it is important to know how one recognizes the difference. How to determine when a family might need referral services in the community needs to be understood.

Another valuable skill for a leader to have is the ability to work with the dynamics of groups. Understanding at what level a group is and helping it move to other levels is a real task; when the group is composed of multi-generations and subgroups of family units, it becomes an even greater task! To a group work leader of adults, a Family Cluster appears large when it contains twenty-five to thirty individuals; but when one considers the strength of the subgroupings of families, a Family Cluster group of four or five family units is not too big. The dynamics are just more complex. It helps if a leader is knowledgeable about:

- dynamics at work in families, as small groups;
- how each family affects the cluster group;
- how the cluster group affects each family group;
- the effects of the leaders on the group;
- the effects of the marriage relationships of couples on the group;
- effects of other subgroups on the cluster, i.e., adolescents, the females, the males, the couples, etc.

Since the Family Cluster Model is an educational one, and the agenda grows out of the group's needs and concerns, it is imperative that a leader know how to design and plan for this process. The experiential mode suggests that a leader be aware of the needs of individuals and the group and learn various ways to collect data about those needs. The leader will need to learn to design a plan which will fit all generations, to be acquainted with a wide repertoire of experiences, and to be flexible. It is helpful to use methods which can facilitate families to change, thereby developing awareness of the spiral effect of this growth mode of education. They should be able to facilitate evaluation and learn to use suggestions from evaluations to design the next sessions. There are a number of books which contain growth exercises, but the secret is to know which exercise to choose and to adapt it to a particular group at its particular stage of growth. This approach cannot be set down recipe-style in a book; rather, one must be cognizant of many facets of leadership and weave them into a fabric of growth for each individual cluster.

Basic to the knowledge each leader should possess is a belief/theology process which combines articulation and behavior; that is, the words and the actions of the leader must be congruent. The belief system must belong to the person and not be an adapted ecclesiastical form nor an inauthentic one. Existential theology suggests that a person's beliefs grow out of his or her experiences, so that they are valid for that individual. This stance is very different from that assumed by many churches, inasmuch as the person has the experience, is authentic in his or her manner of sharing those experiences, and has freedom to develop beliefs out of those experiences. This suggests flexibility toward others on the part of the leader while maintaining a trust and security from one's own belief system.

The skill of such a leader exhibits itself in allowing differences to be expressed and affirmed while also encouraging changes to be accepted. I recall one father telling me that participation in a cluster allowed him to feel freedom from guilt for the first time in that particular church. The cluster accepted him and his belief system as a part of himself; as a result, the person began to have a deepening faith because of the freedom he had to believe. Faith promotes growth when allowed to be free and unhampered. Virginia Satir suggests that an authentic person has a "flowing" or "leveling" way of communicating whereby "the voice says words that match the facial expression, the body position, and voice tone. Relationships are easy, free and honest, and there are few threats to self-esteem." She goes on to say that "only the leveling [response] has any chance to heal ruptures, break impasses, or build bridges between people." The leveling response represents a truth about the person at a moment in time so that "there is an integration, a flowing, an aliveness, an openness and what I call a *juiciness* about a person who is leveling."

> What the leveling response does is make it possible for you to live as a whole person—real, in touch with your head, your heart, your feelings, and your body. Being a leveler, enables you to have integrity, commitment, honesty, intimacy, competence, creativity, and the ability to work with real problems in a real way.[8]

To me, being a leveler also means being a person in faith who communicates this to others and brings forth the reality of faith in the other. Jesus communicated his faith in a "leveling" way, and John describes it when he says: "The Word became a human being and, full of grace and truth, lived among us" (John 1:14, TEV).

At some point in a group's life, it is important to ritualize group beliefs, so persons have a physical manifestation of the group's faith system. Such rituals can be changed when they are no longer valid for the persons' belief systems. In other words, rituals are utilized because of their present relevance to the group's way of living and not because of their past adherence to tradition. This need was exemplified in the first cluster held in a Jewish synagogue; the young Jewish families wanted to instill a faith system in their children but did not find the traditional ways of the synagogue meaningful in today's world. A part of the cluster activities was devoted to developing rituals which were meaningful to the families in the group and relevant to their faith stance. This is a very different approach to traditional religion and appears to be more appropriate for a world of change. It also permits the "spirit of the person" to be acknowledged and expressed. I believe this opens the wellsprings of health and growth in human beings as well as human systems which make religion health producing and creative. A cluster leader will utilize a number of creative activities in the development of rituals: writing, song making, dance, movement, poetry, and others. Some denominations and faiths have established rituals and forms which they believe are important for a family group to follow. To help individuals and families grow in a faith process, it is important for them to have some understanding of their meaning so they can be used with authenticity. One beauty of the cluster model is that it can be used by any group and be adapted to fit any faith and liturgy.

The traditional historical approach to theology is used and validated when the group seeks to find what others have believed in the past, how beliefs have been expressed in biblical tradition, as well as in traditions of other faiths. Many times the adults in the cluster become aware of truths in the Scriptures through reflection on some family experience. The leader may serve as the "translator" between the valid personal experience and biblical words which have the same meaning. Sometimes children will express insights which, when translated into theological language, open new doors of understanding. It is this insight and "spiritual moment" from which children grow in their personal belief systems by glimpsing meanings of importance to the persons who are most significant to their lives. This is religious education at its best.

One exercise often used in the study of faith is the "trust walk" where an adult is paired with a child. The gist of the exercise is that each partner takes the other on a walk of trust, with one guiding and the other closing one's eyes. The leader of the pair is to keep the partner from danger and introduce the partner to as many new experiences as possible. It is amazing how some parents do not trust their own children and have a new awareness of their integrity when the children conduct them safely on the walk. This experience usually provokes intense discussion and confrontation of the meaning of religious trust and how that is modeled in the family. Sometimes it is the children who model trust, and they become the teachers of the adults; all are part of a faith pilgrimage together. David Duncombe states that "there is good reason to believe that Protestant theology must be understood behaviorally before it is adequately understood theoretically. Reflection on the nature of human behavior shows why this is so."[9] To be existentially aware of faith, a leader should be aware of:

- one's own belief system and the values it teaches;
- how that belief system is put into behavioral operation to provide modeling for the others in the group;
- respect for the belief systems of others;
- ways to help others articulate their belief systems;
- the transmission of word meanings from one faith to another;
- the developmental processes of persons in belief systems;
- ritual forms which can be used to express belief systems;
- the dignity and worth of human beings in the universe.

Training for Cluster Leadership

The basic principles for learning to lead a Family Cluster (or any other enrichment group) stem from learning about one's own family and how it is enriched; therefore, training opportunities should provide for the presence of families. Virginia Satir believes that people who are trying to do family work need to understand and relate to their own family; so people who are learning to become family workers need to bring their own families to the process of training.[10] This form of training is known as the laboratory method, first developed by the National Training Laboratory at Bethel, Maine. Since 1972, Family Cluster Training Laboratories have been held in various settings across the North American continent.[11] They are usually sponsored by judicatories, denominations, retreat centers, graduate schools, or ecumenical groupings. These laboratories have several components:

1. A "Family Cluster" component, meeting twice a day for a total of four or five hours. A lab may have one to four cluster groups meeting simultaneously, depending on facilities and sponsorship.
2. A leadership training component, composed of membership in a cluster, skill shops for learning skills important to cluster leadership, and theory sessions.
3. Design planning teams where persons-in-training have an opportunity to design (plan) for a cluster session, lead the session, and critique their performance.

4. Skilled staff which lead clusters for the first three sessions and model leadership of group building and contracting. They serve as resource persons to the design teams and observe when the persons-in-training are leading the clusters. Staff members also facilitate the personal growth of an individual, or help those in a marriage/family relationship be aware of their own dynamics. Staff members need to be fully aware of their own processes of interrelating as well as those of families and groups, to integrate successfully all the components of a one-week, intensive lab.

5. A director who assumes responsibility for the overall coordination of the lab, leads the skill shops, resources the staff, and is a specialist in leading family groups.

Highly skilled persons are available to direct labs and to lead cluster sessions. In describing the most productive kind of training for persons in the helping professions, Robert Carkhuff states:

> The most effective programs appear to be those that (1) focus upon primary facilitative and action-oriented dimensions complemented by secondary dimensions involving potential preferred modes of treatment and (2) integrate the didactic, experiential and modeling aspects of learning.[12]

His work shows these to be the most effective for training through experiential and empirical indexes. The laboratory training model for cluster leadership focuses on:

1. Primary facilitation of families in residence;
2. Primary facilitation of the leaders-in-training;
3. An action-oriented dimension whereby leaders-in-training plan, lead, and evaluate cluster sessions;
4. The integration of cognitive theory with experience;
5. The integration of experiential work with families in clusters;
6. The modeling of skilled leaders at work with families in the beginning of a lab cluster and in supervision of the leaders-in-training while they are working with families in clusters;
7. A highly integrative combination of all facets of the lab, the staff, the families, the clusters, the leaders-in-training, and the personnel related to the site of the lab.

At the conclusion of a lab, usually a person has undergone enough skill practice and training to begin leadership of a cluster. Carkhuff states, "The level of the counselor-trainer's functioning appears to be the single most critical aspect of effective training."[13] The lab model of training appears to be consistent throughout in fostering growth and change for everyone involved in the process.

By 1973, a number of people were requesting shorter-range training than the one-week residential laboratory school; therefore, a workshop format of thirty hours was developed to provide the most basic, primary training for leadership of Family Clusters. The training workshop consists of:

1. Skill shops in which persons-in-training learn necessary skills;
2. Theory input;
3. Two or three demonstrations with families which trainers design;
4. Consideration of next steps in training for participants;
5. Time for questions.

It is apparent that the training workshop is limited; so participants are encouraged to try cluster leadership and then to attend a week-long laboratory school for further understanding and skill building which are necessary to be an effective leader. Training laboratories and workshops are held in various parts of the United States and Canada, and information can be obtained from Family Clustering, Inc.[14]

Many other kinds of workshops offer to provide skills and knowledge of a specialized nature which can enhance a cluster leader's training. These workshops are offered at community colleges, private growth centers, adult education schools, mental health and social work agencies, schools of continuing education, the Association for Creative Change within Religious and Other Social Systems,[15] and others. Some areas of skills are:

1. *Human relations:*
   Interpersonal skills, self-understanding, communication skills, human sexuality, counseling skills, transactional analysis, personal growth;
2. *Family understanding:*
   How families operate within systems, developmental cycles of families, family sociology courses, family therapy, family learning, understanding of one's family of origin, multi-family therapy, family networks;
3. *Group work:*
   Small group leadership, group dynamics, intergenerational groups;

4. *Learning and education:*
   Design skills for experiential education, the learning process, human growth and development;
5. *Theology and beliefs:*
   Process theology, belief practices, values clarification, moral education and development, religious and faith development, belief practices, experiential or behavioral theology.

An advanced group for Family Cluster leaders often is held in the summer at Five Oaks Christian Workers Centre[16] in conjunction with the Family Cluster Training Laboratory. Usually this is composed of persons who have attended a lab and led clusters, and participation is by invitation. It provides further learning in regard to families, leading family groups, and learning the process of training others.

The Process of Training Others

Any person who wishes to train others for the task of Family Cluster leadership must be cognizant of the following:

- the dynamics of leading family growth groups;
- the knowledge and skills important in leading family growth groups;
- the influence of one's family of origin in relating to families;
- ways to divide the knowledge and skills into training components;
- the kind of staff needed and their necessary skills;
- the dynamics of guiding persons-in-training through the training components.

Persons interested in training others should first attend a laboratory school and then lead several clusters so as to gain varied experiences. Then they should go through a learning sequence of training in the following fields:

self-understanding, the leadership role, design skills, group dynamics, understanding of family systems, experiential theology, and observation.

After these experiences, consultants from Family Clustering, Inc. appraise persons to see if they are ready to colead a training experience with a more skilled person. Through apprenticeship a person often is ready to colead a cluster in a training lab.

Studies in Leadership Styles

In 1975 James Call made a study of leadership styles as identified by Richard Monroe in *Exploring Leadership Styles.*[17] These are:

The Directive Style	(designated leader is central and in control of the program)
The Non-Directive Style	(the participants are central and in control of the program)
The Collaborative Style	(mutuality between the leader and participants' roles in the program)
The Corroborative Style	(meeting individual needs out of self-awareness and existentialism in the program).

Through interviewing eight cluster leaders in two different sectors of the country, Call discovered that those leaders found the Collaborative and Corroborative styles most compatible with Family Cluster dynamics in their leadership of clusters. These findings would seem to coincide also with the general philosophy of the model. The Non-Directive style was least compatible with the model and leadership patterns. His study encompassed the Family Cluster Model, the Home Curriculum (Disciples of Christ), Family (Paulist Press), and Lent-Easter Programs (Glenmary Religious Education Center).[18]

As the Family Cluster Model evolves, there will probably be a need for some kind of standard setting for leadership. This is difficult, at best, for any profession or group; it is even more difficult for leadership in a new type of growth group emerging from the dynamics of families. Professional leadership in our culture usually rests on accreditation, standard achievement, and competence. Robert Dow has suggested a trilogy approach to leadership in the church with these categories:

Trainer/Educator—	for information and process
Therapist/Practitioner—	for correction and caring/custody
Theologian/Prophet—	for motivation and sustenance of meaning.[19]

Certain skills could be assessed along this continuum for a leader of family groups:

The Trainer—	who knows the advantages of certain information and skills for families;

The Educator—   who knows how information is learned and
                    how to guide families to learn skills and
                    theory;

The Practitioner—   who knows how to provide caring and
                    protection and helps others to do so;

The Theologian—   who knows how to motivate persons for
                    growth and understands methods to effect
                    change within a belief system;

The Prophet—   who knows how to help persons find meaning
                    for themselves, their family system, and how
                    to apply these to the wider society.

These modes coincide with skills necessary for leading a cluster and provide a framework for the enriching of families through the context of caring, modeling, teaching, belonging, and growing. Such a progression would enable both lay and professional leaders to be models to parents and other adults who would, in turn, be able to influence the younger members of the congregation. All would be "spiritual growth enablers" in a religious community.

Of the family enrichment models listed in chapter 3, those which offer training are designated within the description of the models. Some do not offer specific training to enhance leadership in the model, but rather encourage persons to go through the experience. Others may provide orientation *about* the model but do not train persons to use the model. Simplified models usually assume that anyone interested can lead a family group.

Family groupings possess many dynamics which influence leadership while various kinds of leaders and their leadership styles influence the families in a group. Some of the dynamics to be considered are:

- the power base of individuals in each family and how it is expressed;
- the power dynamics between individuals in a family, i.e., husband/wife, parents/children, siblings, coalitions;
- the power struggles between various family units, i.e., male/female, old/young, adult/child or adolescent, family placement;
- the play hierarchy developed among children;
- the peer group hierarchy developed among the adolescents;
- the perceived power of the leaders, and the leaders' sense of their power;

- the process used by the leaders during the cluster sessions;
- the cultural influence of the socioeconomic structure of the families in the group;
- the investment the individuals and families have in the sponsoring agency, and its effect on the cluster.

Often these factors can be used for the growth of the group; sometimes they serve to hinder a group. It behooves a leader to know about self, families, and groups to be able to utilize their forces. Then the leader must be able to diagnose what is needed, be able to do it or help others to do it, and feel safe in doing it. "An effective leader is one who can behave comfortably along the whole range of leadership styles and who . . . is flexible enough so that his behavior helps the group move toward its goal." [20]

CHAPTER 7

The Continuing Challenge
of Family Enrichment

When Family Clusters were first started, sometimes I was asked, "Is this another fad which will soon pass?" It appears that the family is now beginning to be considered seriously because of the impact that it has on American society. There is much conversation and speech making about the need to consider the family; more realistic action is needed in terms of working with family groups. Within the next decade the challenge will be to discover ways to help the family unit fulfill its potential without taking away its basic rights. Every institution in society is influenced by the family and the manner in which it operates. However, little is done to assist the family in its task of producing mature, stable citizens. It is like a one-way street. Many social institutions and government agencies are moving down the street, taking emotional toll from families, but there does not seem to be a way of return service to the family in the form of support and renewal. If a family manages to cope and survive, it does not receive much recognition for contributing to the society. In order to create healthy, well-integrated individuals, the society must provide support and care for the family unit which best fulfills this task.

Adaptations of the Family Cluster Model

Adaptations of the Family Cluster have attempted to help specific families receive support and care at various periods of their development. To deal with holiday pressures, the *Family Festival Cluster* was developed in 1973 by Rev. Richard Murdoch for use in a small Presbyterian parish in upstate New York. The emergence of the cluster was an outgrowth of his concern that more counseling was needed among parishioners during the Advent and Christmas season. They seemed to have greater despair and depression at that time. In the Sunday worship service he shared the message of hope and joy with those same parishioners, but felt that simply sharing the liturgy did not promote congruence in family living. While conducting further research, he discovered that secular counseling agencies experienced increased caseloads also at the Christmas season. From this concern, he developed the Family Festival Cluster to integrate theological themes and holiday values for more congruent behavior in families as an alternative to stress patterns. The families' evaluative responses showed some movement toward congruency in behavior with their perception of the Christmas message. One year later, in a series of interviews at the 1974 Christmas season, there was evidence of more integration of the theological message with family values which affected the behavior of the families as they celebrated. Murdoch reports that ". . . the Family Festival Clusters were found to be religious resources in learning to behave theologically and in giving Christian witness in a pluralistic culture."[1]

Many families experience camping trips during the summer vacation period. Some churches utilize time at a camp or retreat setting to provide fellowship and recreation for families within a Christian setting. St. Margaret's United Church of Kingston, Ontario, sponsored a five-day *Family Cluster Canoe Trip* in one of the provincial parks. Five family units participated, comprised of seventeen persons, the children ranging from six to fourteen years. All shared in the experience of canoeing, portaging, making camp, and preparing meals. The leaders, John and B. J. Klassen, said this of the experience:

> . . . it was . . . a family cluster marked with reality and commitment scarcely seen in a local church or residential situation. . . . Our holiday following the canoe trip was a continuation of new patterns of operation in relating to one another, taking responsibility, and showing concern for each other.[2]

In 1977 and 1978 a *Family Cluster Camp* was held at Five Oaks Christian Workers' Centre at Paris, Ontario. The purpose of such a camp, as developed by the staff, was ". . . for families to experience the joy of living together by affirming strengths and trying new life styles through using the Family Cluster Model."[3]

Several families had attended a family camp in previous years, so interviews were held to assess reactions about the differences between the two styles of family camping. The majority of the family members of all ages felt they learned more about their families and grew from the experience in the 1977 camp. Often family camps are that only by name, with little emphasis on strengthening the family system or improving family interactions. An authentic "family growth camp" can provide affirmation, skill learning, and behavioral change as the family lives together beyond the camp setting. A doctoral project on the various types of family camping is presently in progress.[4] The possibility of intentional family enrichment is tremendous for use in state parks, at private campgrounds and retreat centers, and within the National Park Ministry program. This type of family enrichment has wide potential for attracting the family not connected with a specific congregation.

Use of the Family Cluster has been made with Jewish congregations and named the *Mishpacha* by Dr. Dov Elkins.[5] The *Mishpacha* shares some similarities with the family *havurot* of Jewish tradition but is distinctive by its use of the family system as its prime teaching medium. The *Mishpacha* was established to further Jewish family life, to provide a time of celebration together, and to foster the formation of surrogate extended families. The attrition of the Jewish community is partly accountable by the diminishing influence of family life among those of the Jewish faith. Mervin Riseman has said this is due, in part, to the decrease in intentional family interaction among Jewish families and in intergenerational socializing, as well as less emphasis on the Jewish aspects of family events.[6] Presently a three-year study is being conducted to examine how family patterns in society at large are affecting Jewish families.

Another group of families affected by the economic and bureaucratic system in which they live are those involved in the *military systems*. There have been a number of Family Clusters held within various military branches, and a pilot Family Cluster Training Workshop was held at Fort Wadsworth, Staten Island, New York, in 1976.[7] Some of the evaluative comments stressed the necessity for support systems among military families. There is need for a well-developed laboratory training experience for chaplains and other leaders to have well-trained enablers of family education within the branches of the military.

Families of the clergy is another unique group of families who have benefitted from Family Cluster adaptation. Often these families feel they have nowhere to turn when they are under stress. Many clergy do not feel they can share family problems with parishioners, yet clergy families need a group in which they can share their concerns. Pilot experiences have been held in Ontario, Canada,[8] and Philadelphia, Pennsylvania.[9] The advantages of having clergy participate with their families in an enrichment event are:

1. Clergy learn how the Model works by seeing it function, firsthand, with their own family.
2. Clergy are made more aware of the potent needs for family education in a parish.
3. The "mystique" related to the clergyperson and his or her family can be explored and dealt with in a caring group.
4. Breakdown in the clergy family can be noted in advance, and referral made to counseling agencies.
5. Clergy can be motivated more easily to obtain further training in leadership of the Model.

This Model could also be adapted for use with the families of seminarians and lay deaconates who are living in a particular situation because of the theological training of one of the parents. Continuing education for clergy could be enhanced with this empirical approach to family education. Through the use of a family systems-based model with their own families, a new awareness could be developed for providing family enrichment in churches. Rev. Donald Conroy, Representative for Family Life of the United States Catholic Conference, has said:

> . . . first is the need for a genuine, thoroughly developed concept of family life ministry. The understanding of the family life apostolate (duties) within the church demands a specialized ministry and training. . . . Instead of more "stop-gap, half-way, or band-aid type of programs" we need "total family life programming" based on a theology and developmental psychology of the maturing Christian family.[10]

It would appear that other types of family units could benefit from family enrichment, such as families of professionals, families of corporate executives who move a great deal, or families of sales personnel who travel a great deal.

The Family Cluster is adaptable to *educational settings* such as parochial schools, private schools, schools for specialized needs, and public schools. The Christian Day School in Waterbury, Connecticut, is adapting clusters for use with families of children in the school. Their emphasis in the school setting is on "established controls that lead toward trust, responsibility, self-control, and genuine love relationships."[11] The purpose of clusters is to provide a structure in which parents and children can also experience the same type of relationship.

There have been three adaptations of the Family Cluster to the *public school setting*. The first was conducted in 1970 with underachieving black children and their families in a Cleveland neighborhood school. A social worker, Marjorie Johnson, became aware of the need to work with family units to facilitate the children's learning process. Through pre- and post-testing, the results from the Cleveland pilot were able to be specified:

1. There was a significant increase in scores relating to personal and social skills of the children.
2. There was a significant increase in reading scores of the children.
3. The families involved created a more positive climate of trust and openness among themselves, leading to increased interaction.
4. The parents, grandparents, and other significant adults expressed interest in the learning experiences of the children.
5. Families discovered some of their family strengths.
6. A number of myths about learning and schools were dispelled.
7. Parents have become more involved in the school after undergoing the experience.[12]

In 1977, a shortened pilot experience was held in a Rochester, New York, city school within a black neighborhood, through the influence of a classroom teacher, Estella Watkins, and a school social worker, Doris Morgan. After meeting a few times, those families provided positive evaluations of their experience.[13] In the spring of 1978, a residential retreat of two weekends was held with families which have children in an integrated neighborhood school in Rochester. One section of the evaluation deals with improvement in interaction between black and white families. Another section deals with strengthening family life through promoting interracial, intergenerational support groups for families. An evaluation was provided by social psychologist Lucinda Sangree and Margaret Sawin.[14] The project was funded through an agency of the Genesee Ecumenical Ministries of Rochester in cooperation with the Rochester City School District.

Educators have become aware of the impact of self-concept on the learning process within the child; seldom has the family unit been used as a teaching force for improving self-concept. Most remedial help for children is based on the "identified client" concept; therefore, the impact of the family system on the individual child has been overlooked. The contribution of the family system to self-worth is the most essential ingredient in a child's personality development and in learning patterns. Virginia Satir says:

> . . . I am convinced that the crucial factor in what happens both *inside* people and *between* people is the picture of individual worth that each person carries around with him. . . .
> I am convinced that there are no genes to carry the feeling of worth. *It is learned.* And the family is where it is learned. . . .
> . . . high-pot parents are more likely to create nurturing families, and low-pot parents troubled families.[15]

Presently the Family Cluster Model is being utilized to bring one-parent families and their children together in a pilot led by Lillian Merry in the First Unitarian Church of Rochester. Bruce Brillinger of the Dellcrest Children's Centre of Toronto, Canada, has been using the Family Cluster as an enrichment form for those families in counseling with social agencies in Toronto. He reports that many of the adults say the experience was the first time they were treated with esteem and their family unit affirmed. Today, many adults need affirmation and caring at the same time their children do; cluster can provide such a place for meeting this need.

Since the model has so much adaptability, it could be used with families having special concerns such as alcohol abuse, drug dependency, and others. These types of families need enrichment and enhancement with therapy and intervention during their long reeducating process.

The Development of Family Life Centers

Our culture, with its emphasis on the individual and the peer group, has not invested energy and money in the family systems approach within the community. Moreover, many programs of family life are based on pathology and counseling instead of prevention and enrichment. One enrichment-oriented center is "Family Place"[16] located in a working-class community of Vancouver, British Columbia. During the writing of her doctoral dissertation on parent education, Clare Buckland became aware that family education must include the complete family as a unit. With a grant proposal in one hand and an embryonic idea in the other, Buckland facilitated the staff, program, and clientele of this storefront, drop-in Family Center. "Some days we have 60–80 children and 50 adults dropping in for relief from the isolation and frustration that all too often beset young mothers. We're relieved to see the model becoming accepted, and two other centers now operating in Vancouver."[17]

Three churches of which I know have instituted Family Life Centers or Institutes. Others have such possibilities under consideration. One of the best known is the Family Life Center of St. Mary of the Lake Roman Catholic parish in suburban Minneapolis. The educational philosophy of the center is built on a growth/learning base with family groupings and community services. Another family-oriented center is that of St. Martin de Pores Roman Catholic parish in Phoenix, Arizona. Located in a low-income section of the city, the center ministers to all types of family needs with a variety of services. The First Baptist Church of Cleveland, Ohio, also has set up a Family Life Institute, ministering to a variety of family needs. The Marylhurst Education Center of Portland, Oregon, established a Family Education Center through the efforts of Sr. Jeanette Benson. A variety of events have been held for families, as well as training events for leaders of family growth groups.[18]

Margaret Mead has suggested that we need more intergenerational interactions in order truly to develop caring for all persons in our society.[19] Edward Thornton wrote that shopping malls need to have religious resource centers which would offer a variety of ministries on an ecumenical basis by professional specialists.[20] One form of ministry could be family enrichment. If such were developed, there would need to be a new focus on funding and support from the community. Community Education Centers could provide a new type of service to family groups within their ongoing programs.

A few universities and professional groups have appropriated vacation and professional conference times as those to which people could bring their families.[21] The possibility of utilizing such periods for intentional family learning experiences is a tremendous option for professional societies to consider. Training components could be built into university programs via the laboratory method to train those persons who wish to become "family facilitators" or "family enablers" in their communities. An added contribution would be that the education institution of the university could serve as a model for facilitating family life in today's society.

A New Mission for Churches

Every neighborhood in America has churches, and most churches have untapped space. A new mission for churches in the last decades of the twentieth century would be to provide neighborhood Family Enrichment Centers. If a church met the family needs of the neighborhood or of its own constituency, it could develop a unique ministry at various points of change within the family cycle. Clinebell states that it is more productive to help the nurturing of "normal" people throughout the family life cycle. This means investing at least three times as much caring time and leadership in person building and human enrichment activities as that spent in counseling those with deep deficiencies.[22] What might a ministry encompass to help the family in its developing cycles?

Premarital workshops and experiences would be available, but the greater emphasis would be on neo-married relationships. Here persons could work on their marriage or couple relationship at its most strategic beginning in regard to communication skills, conflict resolution, use of money and resources, sexual behaviors, relationships to in-laws, differing belief and value systems, and the use of crisis points as growth possibilities. Periodic marital checkups could be utilized with personality instruments, peer counseling groups, and professional counseling where needed.

At the birth of the first child, parents would have an opportunity for workshops in parenting, development of personality and religious attitudes, and skills in early child rearing. Strategic to a person's process of learning is the developmental period from seven to thirty-six *months* of age. Just as important are the religious attitudes developed at that time which include trust, risk, commitment, and love. The importance of self could be emphasized with the young child as well as with the parents as they are moving through their own adult developmental stages. All kinds of possibilities emerge for parent education as a child passes through different developmental stages.

Periodically, couples would be involved in marriage enrichment to enhance their own relationship. Problems and concerns could be dealt with before they reached crisis proportions. A realistic prevention approach would be operative. This would provide an opportunity for parents to intentionalize working on their own relationship while integrating the demands of young children within the family system.

Family enrichment would become a reality as the young child moved into the neighborhood play group, for it is here that the pressures of peer groups are first felt. Families could also begin to consider their value systems at the time the child is being influenced by the bombardment of value pressures from the television. This experience would enable the young family to be aware of its strengths, its potential, and its limitations. It could begin to work in skill areas which would facilitate the intermingled relationships of the family system. A family also could begin to consider its belief system in relation to its behaviors and how they may be made more congruent. As children develop into adolescents, the "value collision period" could be better understood and handled. Crises in family relationships could be considered before they reached momentous proportions.

Other points of crisis could be addressed through periodic support groups. Such opportunities might be considered around "middlelesence," adolescence, divorce or separation, aging parents, vocational changes, retirement and change in life-style, life as a single person, death and the grieving process, special concerns of men and women, and others.

Within its own clientele, the church has persons from birth to death; thus it is the one institution which could readily provide intergenerational activities. Such experiences would allow persons from different ages and dissimilar eras of living to have more understanding. John H. Westerhoff III states that "true community necessitates the presence and interaction of three generations." [23] The older generation is the one of tradition and memory. The middle-age generation is that of the present, dealing with everyday questions of "here and now." The youngest generation is the one of vision and hope. It is only as we have all three generations together can we expect to have a Christian community adequate for faith in the space age.

A church which believes in social action and community involvement must be aware of the family's impact on the community through the manner it teaches its individual members to interact with others and with institutions in the society. Virginia Satir has suggested that we must start with the family system in order to promote caring and nurturing among other groups in the society. In her assessment of social interaction, she has listed the following priorities:

1. The most important area of family life is the development and continuation of *self-worth*. This is the foundation block for the individual, for the family, and for the society.
2. Sharing the meanings of life's experiences is the prime purpose

for interacting. The manner in which persons interact is related to how they share in verbal and nonverbal communication. We cannot share meanings until first we communicate effectively.

3. The process people use for acting out their meanings, as well as for accomplishing tasks, is related to the way in which power is used and controlled. This is reflected in the rules and order of the family. The actions of a family reflect their beliefs and accommodation to the power issues.

4. The above three points, as lived out in a family, provide the foundation for individuals to live in the society. "And when these powerful forces start to function in your family, making it a more nurturing one, these same kinds of forces will be applied in society. It could even be the beginning of a new kind of society. After all, the family unit is the synthesizing link to its parent—society as a whole."[24]

Families provide the yeast for behavior within society's institutions.

John Westerhoff states that a faith community possesses a clear identity, intimacy of a small group, intergenerational contacts, and role diversity.[25] The theological principals of a faith community are inherent in the Family Cluster. A cluster of families establishes its identity with the contract and the surfacing of important issues for the people involved in the cluster. The cluster is small and shares some of the intimacies which are inherent within family life. Because of its familial nature, it is intergenerational. It acknowledges the humanness of all persons within its membership, thus allowing each person freedom to grow and to become. This belief is carried over to the family system in which the individual lives, allowing for families to share more freedom and creativity. The autonomy and growth of an individual are reinforced by the family system. The family system provides security and trust from which the individual can depart to risk and explore. The cluster provides the covenant community which supports the family while encouraging it to change and grow. Together, the families make an extended "faith family" for modeling and experimenting. This kind of family living develops "many threads" to exist and to cope creatively in a fast-changing society. The authors of *No Single Thread* have made explicit how such a family is a more productive, healthy one.[26] Religious educator James Michael Lee has said that "the only authentic family-centered religious education is one which involves the total family qua family. Family-centered religious education is the most natural, the most pervasive, the most personalistic, and the most effective of all forms of religious education."[27]

A cluster family in the United Congregational Church of Kingston, Rhode Island, went on sabbatical to Perth, Australia, which is the most geographically isolated city in the world. While visiting a Methodist church the first Sunday, they heard an announcement that there was need for families to start a Family Cluster.

> They were both astonished and warmed by the ties that bind us together—across the oceans—in Family Clusters within the church family. The message is getting out, and your work in Australia has circled the globe via a young family in their first weeks in a new country.[28]

Social psychiatrist E. Manswell Pattison has suggested that the church has four distinct functions to contribute to the total sociocultural milieu of society.[29] The church is a *valuing center* which promotes positive goals and commitment to values, along with dialogue in regard to changing values. While doing so, it values the life of each human being with the affirmation that he or she is valued unconditionally by the Creator. The church is a *learning/growth center* during the lifetime of developmental cycles. It helps persons grow toward their potential and learn ways of doing this experientially. It also helps families realize their collective strengths in order to release potential for growth at normal crises in the developmental cycles. The church is a *sustaining/maintaining* center. It can provide intimate, nurturing groups at a time the society needs more sustaining, security-giving experiences. The church is a *restoration center* to assist in the repair of broken relationships. The Family Cluster provides an opportunity for the church to find genuine expression of these functions. An eight-year-old expressed her feelings about membership in a cluster in the following manner:

> Family Cluster:
> Together,   Joyful
> Doing,   Singing,   Talking
> I am happy here.
> Unity.
>
> —*Amy Maynard*[30]

Possible Questions for a Data Collector

To Be Used in Planning Family Clusters

POSSIBLE QUESTIONS FOR A DATA COLLECTOR
To be used in planning for FAMILY CLUSTERS

(This questionnnaire is for *everyone* in the family to fill out. Preschool children can dictate their answers. This will help us plan for the Family Clusters from the kinds of answers each member of the family gives. Please return by _____to _____ .)

1. What have you had the most fun doing in your family?

2. What do you like about your family?

3. What "bugs" you about your family?

4. What are some subjects (or ideas, information) which you think your family needs to talk about?

5. What subjects are never talked about in your family?

6. What are some subjects you'd prefer *not* to have your family talk about?

7. Whom do you feel you are most like in your family?

8. What is most important in your life?

9. What would you like to have happen because you and your family are in a Family Cluster together?

10. Have you answered these questions honestly?

Name _____

Grade in
Age _____ school _____

Hobby _____

Addresses

A. Family Growth Groups

1. The Family Cluster, developed by Margaret Sawin
    Family Clustering, Inc.
    P. O. Box 18074
    Rochester, NY 14618

2. The Family Cluster, developed by Herbert Otto—described in
the book, *The Family Cluster: A Multi-Base Alternative* which
can be obtained from:
    Holistic Press
    160 South Robertson Blvd.
    Beverly Hills, CA 90211
   Dr. Herbert Otto can be reached at:
    222 Westbourne St.
    La Jolla, CA 92037

3. The Family Actualization Model, developed by Anne Lee
Kreml
    Ms. Anne Lee Kreml
    Nebraska Conference of the United Church of Christ
    2055 E. Street
    Lincoln, NE 68510

4. The Family Camp, developed by Ed Branch
    Mr. Ed Branch
    The Hyphen Consultants, Ltd.
    10022 103rd Street
    Edmonton, Alberta
    Canada

5, The One-Parent Family Camp
> Five Oaks Christian Workers Centre
> Box 216
> Paris, Ontario N3L 3E7
> Canada

6. Family Weekend, developed by Ted Bowman
> Family and Children's Service
> 301 S. Brevard Street
> Charlotte, NC 28202

Ted Bowman can be reached at Family and Children's Services, 414 S. Eighth Street, Minneapolis, MN 55404.

7. Family Enrichment Weekend, developed by Carl Clarke, Russell Wilson, and June Wilson
> Rev. Russell Wilson
> Morningside College
> Sioux City, IA 51106

8. Family Enrichment, developed by the Character Research Project of Union College
> The Character Research Project
> 207 State Street
> Schenectady, NY 12305
> or
> The Association Press
> 291 Broadway
> New York, NY 10007

B. Family Skill Models

1. The process model of Virginia Satir
> Ms. Virginia Satir
> P. O. Box 11457
> Palo Alto, CA 94306

2. Peoplemaking Through Family Communication, developed by Roberts and Berry
> National Family Communication Skills Center
> 3278 Alpine Rd.
> Menlo Park, CA 94025

3. Filial Programs, developed by Bernard Guerney and colleagues
   Division of Individual and Family Studies
   College of Human Development
   Catherine Beecher House
   The Pennsylvania State University
   University Park, PA 16802

4. The Family Enrichment Program, developed by Luciano
   L'Abate and associates—obtainable from:
   Social Research Laboratories
   P. O. Box 20076, Station N
   Atlanta, GA 30325
   Dr. L'Abate can be reached at:
   Family Studies Center
   Georgia State University, University Plaza
   Atlanta, GA 30303

5. The Community Family Workshop, developed by Laurent Roy
   Mr. Laurent Roy
   The Growth Exchange
   53 Exchange Street
   Portland, ME 04111

6. Family Check-Up, developed by Dawn Simon
   Ms. Dawn Simon
   Family and Child Service for Greater Seattle
   500 Lowman Building
   107 Cherry Street
   Seattle, WA 98104

7. Understanding Us, developed by Patrick Carnes
   Family Renewal Center
   Suite B-71
   6545 France Avenue S.
   Edina, MN 55435

8. The Family Class/Workshop, developed by Re-Evaluation
   Counseling
   The Re-Evaluation Counseling Communities
   719 Second Avenue N.
   Seattle, WA 98109

9. Family labs, developed by Breidenbach and Hover
   Full Circle
   4833 West 76th Terrace
   Prairie Village, KS 66208

C. Family-Based Models for Religious Indoctrination

1. Family-Centered Programs, developed by Glenmary Mission-
   ers
   Religious Education Center
   Glenmary Home Missioners
   2501 Ashwood Avenue
   Nashville, TN 37212

2. Families, developed by Maureen Gallagher
   FAMILY Parish Religious Education Program
   Paulist Press
   400 Sette Drive
   Paramus, NJ 07652

3. Family Learning Teams, developed by Mercedes and Joseph
   Iannone
   Family Learning Teams, Inc.
   P. O. Box 42
   Mt. Vernon, VA 22121

4. Family Weekend Experience, developed by Jack and Marcia
   Byington
   W. H. Sadlier
   11 Park Place
   New York, NY 10007
       or
   Worldwide Marriage Encounter Resource Community
   567 Morris Avenue
   Elizabeth, NJ 07208

5. The Mishpacha, developed by Dov Elkins
   Growth Associates
   P. O. Box 8429
   Rochester, NY 14618

6. The Family Havurot, developed by the Reconstructionist Jewish Movement—information obtainable from
   Dr. Bernard Reisman
   Philip W. Lown Graduate Center
   Brandeis University
   Waltham, MA 02154

7. Operation Family, developed by John and Milly Youngberg
   Dr. John Youngberg
   Andrews University
   Berrien Springs, MI 49104

8. Sunday School Plus, developed by Larry Richards
   Renewal Research Associates
   2026 A West Cactus Road
   Phoenix, AZ 85029

9. Kits for Parents, developed by David C. Cook Publishing Co.
   David C. Cook Publishing Co.
   850 N. Grove Avenue
   Elgin, IL 60120

D. Family-Based Models for Recreation and Socializing

1. The Extended Family, developed by the First Unitarian Church of Santa Barbara, California
   The Extended Family
   The First Unitarian Church
   1535 Santa Barbara Street
   Santa Barbara, CA 93101
           or
   The Unitarian-Universalist Association
   25 Beacon Street
   Boston, MA 02108

2. The Family Fun Council, developed by Otto and Kilmer
   Holistic Press
   160 South Robertson Blvd.
   Beverly Hills, CA 90211

Notes

Notes to the Preface

[1] Virginia Satir, *Conjoint Family Therapy,* rev. ed. (Palo Alto, Calif.: Science and Behavior Books, Inc., 1967), p. 182.

Chapter 1

[1] Douglas Andrew Anderson, "Guidelines for the Theory and Practice of the Family Growth Group in the Local Church" (Doctoral dissertation, Boston University Graduate School, April, 1973), p. 62.

[2] Jacques Mousseau, "The Family, Prison of Love" (An interview with Philippe Aries), *Psychology Today* (August, 1975), p. 53.

[3] Richard Farson et al., *The Future of the Family* (New York: Family Service of America, 1969), p. 74.

[4] Anderson, *op. cit.,* pp. 99–101.

[5] Hope Jensen Leichter, "Some Perspectives on the Family as Educator," *Teacher College Record,* vol. 76, no. 2 (December, 1974), p. 175.

[6] Margaret Mead, *Culture and Commitment* (New York: Natural History Press, Doubleday, 1970), p. 58.

[7] "Post-industrial society" was coined by Daniel Bell "to signify a society in which the economy is largely based on service, the professional and technical classes dominate, theoretical knowledge is central, intellectual technology—systems analysis, model building, and the like—is highly developed, and technology is, at least potentially, capable of self-sustaining growth." (Explained in Alvin Toffler, *Future Shock* [New York: Random House, 1970], p. 433.)

[8] Clare M. Buckland, "Toward a Theory of Parent Education: Family Learning Centers in the Post-Industrial Society," *The Family Coordinator,* vol. 21, no. 2 (April, 1972), p. 153.

[9] *Ibid.,* p. 158.

[10] William J. Goode, *The Family* (Englewood Cliffs, N.J.: Prentice-Hall, Inc., 1964), p. 92.

[11] Herbert A. Otto, "Has Monogamy Failed?" *Saturday Review* (April 25, 1970), p. 25.

144 □ Family Enrichment with Family Clusters

[12] Herbert A. Otto, *The Use of Family Strength Concepts and Methods in Family Life Education* (Beverly Hills, Calif.: The Holistic Press, 1975), p. 32.

[13] Jerry M. Lewis, W. Robert Beavers, John T. Gossett, and Virginia Austin Phillips, *No Single Thread: Psychological Health in Family Systems* (New York: Bruner/ Mazel, Publishers, 1976), chapter 9.

[14] David C. Speer, "Family Systems: Morphostasis and Morphogenesis or 'Is Homeostasis Enough?'" *Family Process*, vol. 9 (September, 1970), p. 259.

[15] Virginia Satir, *Peoplemaking* (Palo Alto, Calif.: Science and Behavior Books, Inc., 1972), p. 13, 14.

[16] Mead, *op. cit.,* p. 64.

[17] *Ibid.,* p. 66.

[18] Robert Jay Lifton, "Adaptation and Value Development: Self Process in Protean Man," *The Acquisition and Development of Values: Perspectives in Research* (Bethseda, Md.: National Institute of Child Health and Development, 1968), p. 40. (Report of conference held under the same title.)

Chapter 2

[1] Allen L. Edwards, *Edwards Personal Preference Schedule Manual* (New York: The Psychological Corporation, Inc., 1959).

[2] *Ibid.,* p. 11.

[3] Margaret M. Sawin, "A Study of Sunday Church School Teachers' Personality Characteristics and Attitudes Toward Children" (Doctoral dissertation, University of Maryland, 1969).

[4] *Ibid.,* chapter 2.

[5] Don E. Hamachek, "What Research Tells Us About the Characteristics of 'Good' and 'Bad' Teachers," *Human Dynamics in Psychology and Education* (Boston: Allyn and Bacon, Inc. 1968), p. 190.

[6] A "model is an attempt to symbolize in a practical manner the reality we try to grasp. It is not valid unless it helps us to find meaning, to make sense out of the world. It is not valid unless that meaning can lead us to practical, creative consequences for ourselves and others." From Gordon L. Lippett, *Visualizing Change: Model Building and the Change Process* (Fairfax. Va.: NTL Learning Resources Company, 1973).

[7] "Broken Squares" is found in J. William Pfeiffer and John E. Jones, *A Handbook of Structured Experiences for Human Relations Training,* vol. 5 (La Jolla, Calif.: University Associates, 1969), p. 24.

[8] Louise Fitzhugh and Sandra Scoppetone, *Suzuki Beane* (New York: Doubleday and Company, Inc., 1961).

Chapter 3

[1] Joe Leonard and Richard Gladden, "American Baptist Family Life Education Survey" (Valley Forge, Pa.: A study jointly conducted by four agencies of American Baptist Churches in the U.S.A., 1977), pp. 23, 24, 26, 27, 28.

[2] *Ibid.,* p. 36.

[3] "Plays for Living," Family Service Association of America, 44 E. Twenty-third Street, New York, NY 10010.

[4] For consultants, leaders for family enrichment, or filmstrip on Family Clusters, write Family Clustering, Inc., P. O. Box 18074, Rochester, NY 14618.

[5] John H. Westeroff III, *Will Our Children Have Faith?* (New York: A Crossroad ʔook, imprint of the Seabury Press, Inc., 1976).

[6] Radio interview on "The Family Matters," Station KGO, San Francisco, California, (December 28, 1975).

[7] Larry Wright and Luciano L'Abate, "Four Approaches to Family Facilitation: Some Issues and Implications," *The Family Coordinator,* vol. 26, no. 2 (April, 1977).

[8] Appreciation is due Rev. John Edwards of Adelaide, South Australia, for his contribution in refining the concept of the cluster contract.

[9] Books to use in contracting:

Charles and Ann Morse, *Whobody There?* (Winona, Minn.: St. Mary's College Press, 1971).

Dr. Seuss, *Horton Hears a Who* (New York: Random House, 1954).

Mary Green, *Is It Hard? Is It Easy?* (Reading, Mass.: Addison-Wesley Publishing Company, Inc., 1960).

[10] Games to use in contracting:

BLOCKHEAD, a commercial game produced by the Saalfield Publishing Company, Akron, Ohio.

Andrew Fluegelman, ed., *The New Games Book* (New York: Doubleday, Dolphin Books, 1976).

[11] Lucinda Sangree, "Report and Evaluation of the Family Cluster Laboratory Process" (Written report, December, 1974).

[12] Franz Rosenzweig, Editoral in *Academy Reporter*, vol. 2, no. 6 (June, 1966), p. 1. Quoted in Howard J. and Charlotte H. Clinebell, *The Intimate Marriage* (New York: Harper & Row, Publishers, 1970), p. 185.

[13] A "gestalt" is a pattern in the mind of interrelated structures which make up an experience. Together, these structures are more than the sum of their parts because of their effect on each other, as well as on the total experience. It is exponential in character. The response of a person to a given situation is a total "gestalt" of how he or she has experienced and perceived the situation.

[14] Margaret M. Sawin, Estella Watkins, and Rick Watkins, "Family Clustering: A Way to Grow," *The Associate Reformed Presbyterian*, vol. 1, no. 17 (September, 1976).

Chapter 4

[1] "A system is a complex of elements or parts related in a causal network in a way that each part is related to each other part, plus the whole system in a more or less stable way within a particular time period." From A. D. Hall and R. E. Fagan, "Definition of a System," in Walter Buckley, ed. *Modern Systems Research for the Behavioral Scientist: A Source Book* (Chicago: Aldine Publishing Company, 1968), p. 493.

[2] Anne Lee Kreml, "Understanding Conflict in the Normal Family: An Educational Model for Family Actualization" (Master's thesis, Chicago Divinity School, Chicago, Ill., 1970).

[3] Personal correspondence to the author from Virginia Satir, January 14, 1977.

[4] *Ibid.*

[5] Bernard E. Guerney, Jr. et al., *Relationship Enhancement* (San Francisco: Jossey-Bass Publishers, 1977).

[6] Harvey Jackins, *The Human Side of Human Beings: The Theory of Re-evaluation Counseling* (Seattle: Rational Island Publishers, 1965).

[7] Herbert A. Otto, *Marriage and Family Enrichment: New Perspectives and Programs* (Nashville: Abingdon Press, 1976), p. 25.

[8] Leon Smith, *Family Ministry: An Educational Resource for the Local Church* (Nashville: Division of Education, Board of Discipleship, United Methodist Church, 1975).

[9] Consultant services are available from Family Clustering, Inc., P. O. Box 18074, Rochester, NY 14618.

[10] *Ibid.*

[11] Otto, *op. cit.*, p. 15.

[12] Urie Bronfenbrenner, "We Are Not a Caring Society," *Democrat and Chronicle*, Rochester, N.Y. (November 29, 1976).

Chapter 5

[1] Books which tell of the experiential education process are:
Arthur W. Combs et al., *Perceiving, Behaving, Becoming: A New Focus for Education* (Washington, D.C.: Association for Supervision and Curriculum Development of the National Education Association, 1962).
Robert Arthur Dow, *Learning Through Encounter: Experiential Education in the Church* (Valley Forge, Pa.: Judson Press, 1971).
John Hendrix and Lela Hendrix, *Experiential Education—X/Ed: How to Get Your Church Started* (Nashville: Abingdon Press, 1975).
Malcolm S. Knowles, *Modern Practice of Adult Education: Androgony vs. Pedagogy* (New York: Association Press, 1970).
"Designing for Educational Events," Part III of *Basic Readers in Human Relations Training.* Available from the Episcopal Church, Service to Dioceses, 815 Second Ave., New York, NY 10017.

[2] Margaret M. Sawin, Estella Watkins, and Rick Watkins, "Family Clustering: A Way to Grow," *The Associate Reformed Presbyterian*, vol. 1, no. 17 (September, 1976).

[3] Howard J. Clinebell, Jr., *Growth Counseling for Marriage Enrichment: Pre-Marriage and the Early Years* (Philadelphia: Fortress Press, 1975), p. 5.

[4] Virginia Satir, *Peoplemaking* (Palo Alto, Calif.: Science and Behavior Books, Inc., 1972). The price is $7.95 in hardback, $4.95 in paperback.

[5] Family Clustering, Inc., P. O. Box 18074, Rochester, NY 14618.

[6] *The Purple Turtle*, four issues at the subscription price, $3.50 per year; available from Family Clustering, Inc.

[7] See James H. D. Bossard and Eleanor S. Bell, *Ritual in Family Living* (Philadelphia: University of Pennsylvania Press, 1950).

[8] Rodney W. Napier and Matti K. Gershenfeld, *Groups: Theory and Experience* (Boston: Houghton Mifflin Company, 1973), p. 260.

Chapter 6

[1] Rodney W. Napier and Matti K. Gershenfeld, *Groups: Theory and Experience* (Boston: Houghton Mifflin Company, 1973), p. 138.

[2] *Ibid.*, p. 144.

[3] *Ibid.*, p. 145.

[4] Virginia Satir, *Peoplemaking* (Palo Alto, Calif.: Science and Behavior Books, Inc., 1972), p. 235.

[5] See I. Knickerbocker, "Leadership: A Conception and Some Implications," *Leadership in Action* (Washington, D.C.: National Training Laboratory, 1961) p. 72.

[6] Robert R. Carkhuff, *Helping and Human Relations: A Primer for Lay and Professional Helpers,* vol. 1, *Selection and Training* (New York: Holt, Rinehart and Winston, Inc., 1969), p. 11. Copyright © 1969 by Holt, Rinehart and Winston, Inc. Reprinted by permission of Holt, Rinehart and Winston, Inc.

[7] Robert R. Carkhuff, *Helping and Human Relations: A Primer for Lay and Professional Helpers,* vol. 2, *Practice and Research* (New York: Holt, Rinehart and Winston, Inc., 1969), p. 63. Copyright © 1969 by Holt, Rinehart and Winston, Inc. Reprinted by permission of Holt, Rinehart and Winston, Inc.

[8] Satir, *op. cit.,* pp. 72, 73, 74, 77.

[9] David E. Duncombe, *The Shape of the Christian Life* (Nashville: Abingdon Press, 1969), p. 178.

[10] Virginia Satir, *Y Circulator* (a magazine of the YMCAs), vol. 2, no. 2 (September, 1971).

[11] Margaret M. Sawin, "Planning for a Family Cluster Laboratory Training School," mimeographed paper (1975, rev. 1978).

[12]Carkhuff, vol. 1, *op cit.*, p. 151.

[13]*Ibid.*, p. 157.

[14]Family Clustering, Inc., P. O. Box 18074, Rochester, NY 14618. Tel. (716)244-2008. Send stamped, self-addressed envelope.

[15]The Association for Creative Change within Religious and Other Social Systems, Box 2212, Syracuse, NY 13220. Tel. (315) 424-1802.

[16]Five Oaks Christian Workers Centre, Box 216, Paris, Ontario N3L 3E7, Canada. Tel. (519) 442-3212.

[17]Richard E. Monroe, *Exploring Leadership Styles* (Nashville: Division of Education, Board of Discipleship, the United Methodist Church, 1972).

[18]James Call, "An Exploration of Leadership Styles in Four Intergenerational Programs Designed for the Local Church" (An independent study for the Graduate School, George Peabody College for Teachers, 1975).

[19]Robert Dow, "Trilogy of Leadership: Training, Therapy, Theology" (Mimeographed paper developed for American Baptist Churches in the U.S.A., 1970).

[20]Napier and Gershenfeld, *op. cit.*, p. 164.

Chapter 7

[1]Richard E. Murdoch, "Use of Family Festival Clusters by a Church in Relation to Holiday Stress" (Doctoral project, Colgate-Rochester Divinity School/Bexley Hall/Crozer, Rochester, N.Y., 1975). Condensed in "A Family Festival Cluster," *Religious Education*, vol. 72, no. 5 (September-October, 1977).

[2]B. J. Klassen, "A Report of the Family Cluster Canoe Trip," mimeographed (1974).

[3]Brian Jackson, "Report of the Family Cluster Camp Held at Five Oaks Christian Workers' Centre" (Mimeographed paper available from the author, Hamilton Conference of the United Church of Canada, P.O. Box 100, Carlisle, Ont. LOR 1 HO, Canada, 1977).

[4]Richard Sutton, "A Conceptual Framework of the Family for the Church's Ministry, as Illustrated Through Family Camping" (Doctoral project in process at Colgate-Rochester Divinity School/Bexley Hall/Crozer, Rochester, N.Y.).

[5]Dov Peretz Elkins, "Educating by Families—A New Learning Model," *Humanizing Jewish Life: Judaism and the Human Potential Movement* (Cranbury, N.J.: A. S. Barnes & Company, 1976).

[6]Richard Yaffe, "U.S. Jewish Family Under Pressure," *Jewish Advocate* (December 30, 1976).

[7]Margaret M. Sawin, "Evaluation of the Family Cluster Training Workshop at Fort Wadsworth, Staten Island, New York," mimeographed paper, 1976.

[8]Margaret M. Sawin, "Evaluation of the Wentworth Rural Clergy Family Cluster, Ontario, Canada," mimeographed paper, 1975.

[9]Claude A. Pullis, "The Philadelphia Story: An Assessment of the Five Clergy Families Who Participated in the Clergy Family Enrichment Event, May 29-31, 1976" (Doctoral project in progress at Colgate-Rochester Divinity School/Bexley Hall/Crozer, Rochester, N.Y., 1978).

[10]Fr. Donald Conroy, "Total Family Programming," *Origins: The NC Documentary Service*, vol. 5, no. 21 (November 13, 1975), p. 323.

[11]Personal correspondence with author from Sue Van Natta Smith, head teacher of the Waterbury Christian Day School, 1977. Address: 359 Cooke Street, Waterbury, CT 06710.

[12]Marjorie W. Johnson, "Ile Si Ile (From Porch to Porch): A Program for a Family Learning Experience with a Team Approach" (Unpublished paper submitted to the Pace Association, 518 Arcade, Cleveland, OH 44114, 1970).

[13]Doris Morgan, "Family Cluster—A New Idea for Schools" (Speech delivered at the National Conference of School Social Workers, Denver, Colorado, April, 1978).

[14] Lucinda Sangree and Margaret M. Sawin, "Evaluation of Interracial Clusters Within the Rochester City School District" (1978). Available for $5.00 from Family Clustering, Inc., P. O. Box 18074. Rochester, NY 14618.

[15] Virginia Satir, *Peoplemaking* (Palo Alto, Calif.: Science and Behavior Books, Inc., 1972), pp 21, 24, 27.

[16] Family Place, 2505-2521 Dunbar Street, Vancouver, B.C. V6R 3N4, Canada.

[17] Personal correspondence to the author from Dr. Clare Buckland, 1975.

[18] *Family Life Center,* St. Mary of the Lake, 105 N. Forestview Lane, Minneapolis, MN 55441; *Family Education Programs,* St. Martin de Pores Community Center, 3851 W. Wier Avenue, Phoenix, AR 85041; *Family Life Institute,* The First Baptist Church of Cleveland, 3630 Fairmount Boulevard, Cleveland, OH 44118; *Family Education Center,* Marylhurst Learning Center, Marylhurst, OR 97036. Sr. Jeanette Benson is now Family Education Consultant for the Diocese of Yakima, Washington.

[19] Margaret Mead (Address delivered at the Religious Education Convention, St. Louis, Mo., November, 1977).

[20] Edward E. Thornton, "Ministries of Culture and Counter Culture," *The Journal of Pastoral Care*, vol. 24, no. 2 (June, 1970).

[21] Donald Johnston, "Learning While on Vacation," *The New York Times,* "The Week in Review" (August 19, 1973).

[22] Howard J. Clinebell, Jr., *Growth Counseling for Marriage Enrichment: Pre-Marriage and the Early Years* (Philadelphia: Fortress Press, 1975), p. 4.

[23] John H. Westerhoff III, *Will Our Children Have Faith?* (New York: A Crossroad Book, imprint of the Seabury Press, Inc., 1976), p. 53.

[24] Satir, *op. cit.*, p. 297.

[25] Westerhoff, *op. cit.*, pp. 52-54.

[26] Jerry M. Lewis, W. Robert Beavers, John T. Gossett, and Virginia Austin Phillips, *No Single Thread: Psychological Health in Family Systems* (New York: Brunner/ Mazel, Publishers, 1976).

[27] James Michael Lee, "Toward a New Era: A Blueprint for Positive Action," in James Michael Lee, ed., *The Religious Education We Need: Toward the Renewal of Christian Education* (Mishawaka, Ind.: Religious Education Press, Inc., 1977), p. 115.

[28] Personal correspondence to the author from Rev. Rebecca Erb, Kingston, Rhode Island, November, 1976.

[29] E. Manswell Pattison, "Systems Pastoral Care," *The Journal of Pastoral Care,* vol. 27 (March, 1972), p. 214.

[30] Amy Maynard, quintain written at the Family Cluster Laboratory Training School, Keuka College, New York, 1973.

Bibliography

(Items marked with an asterisk are most useful)

A. **Books which give general background information on faith and culture:**

*Duncombe, David E., *The Shape of the Christian Life*. Nashville: Abingdon Press, 1969.

Hansel, Robert R., *Like Father, Like Son, Like Hell: A Basis for Adult-Youth Understanding*. New York: The Seabury Press, 1969.

James, Muriel, and Savary, Louis M., *The Power at the Bottom of the Well*. New York: Harper and Row, Publishers, 1974.

Maslow, Abraham H., *Values, Religion and Peak Experiences*. New York: Viking Press, Inc., 1970.

*Mead, Margaret, *Culture and Commitment*. Garden City, N.Y.: Natural History Press for the American Museum of Natural History, 1970.

*Toffler, Alvin, *Future Shock*. New York: Random House, 1970.

Westerhoff, John H. III., *Will Our Children Have Faith?* New York: A Crossroad Book, imprint of The Seabury Press, 1976.

B. **For use with chapters 3, 4 and 5 to gain background information on family life:**

Billingsley, Andrew, *Black Families and the Struggle for Survival: Teaching Our Children to Walk Tall*. New York: Friendship Press, 1974.

*Carr, Jo, and Sorley, Imogene, *The Intentional Family.* Nashville: Abingdon Press, 1971.

Christiansen, Harold T., ed, *Handbook of Marriage and the Family.* Chicago: Rand McNally and Company, 1964.

Committee on Ministries with Black Families, Room 711, 475 Riverside Drive, New York, NY 10027.

*Duval, Evelyn Miller, *Family Development.* Philadelphia: J. B. Lippincott, 1967 (third ed.).

Gaulke, Earl H., *You Can Have a Family Where Everybody Wins: Christian Perspectives on Parent Effectiveness Training.* St. Louis: Concordia Publishing House, 1975.

Henry, Jules, *Pathways to Madness.* New York: Random House, 1973.

Hersey, Paul, and Blanchard, Kenneth, *The Family Game: A Situational Approach to Effective Parenting.* Reading, Mass.: Addison Wesley Publishing Company, Inc., 1978.

*Hill, Robert B., *The Strengths of Black Families.* New York: Emerson Hall Publishers, Inc., 1971.

Larson, Lyle E., *The Canadian Family in Comparative Perspective.* Scarborough, Ont.: Prentice-Hall of Canada, 1976.

*Lewis, Jerry M.; Beavers, Robert W.; Gossett, John T.; and Phillips, Virginia Austin, *No Single Thread: Psychological Health in Family Systems.* New York: Brunner/Mazel, Publishers, 1976.

Luckey, Eleanore B., and Wise, George W., *Human Growth and the Family.* Nashville: The Methodist Publishing House, 1970.

McCubbin, Hamilton I.; Dahl, Barbara; and Hunter, Edna J., eds., *Families in the Military System.* Beverly Hills, Calif.: Sage Publications, 1976.

*Otto, Herbert A., ed. *The Family in Search of a Future.* New York: Appleton-Century-Crofts, 1970.

Otto, Herbert A., *Marriage and Family Enrichment: New Perspectives and Programs.* Nashville: Abingdon, 1976.

"Rituals for the Black Family" available from Black Family Rituals, P. O. Box 4956, Philadelphia, PA 19119.

Rubin, Lillian Breslow, *Worlds of Pain: Life in the Working Class Family.* New York: Basic Books, Inc., 1976.

*Satir, Virginia, *Peoplemaking.* Palo Alto, Calif.: Science and Behavior Books, Inc., 1972.

Satir, Virginia; Stachowiak, James; and Taschman, Harvey A., *Helping Families to Change.* New York: Jason Aronson, Inc., 1976.

Skolnick, Arlene S. and Jerome H., eds., *Family in Transition: Rethinking Marriage, Sexuality, Child-Rearing and Family Organization.* Boston: Little, Brown and Company, 1971.

Skolnick, Arlene S. and Jerome H., eds., *Intimacy, Family and Society.* Boston: Little, Brown and Company, 1974.

Wynn, J. C., ed., *Sex, Family and Society in Theological Focus.* New York: Association Press, 1966.

C. For use with chapters 3 and 4—books which interpret family education and how to organize it in churches:

Anderson, Phillip and Phoebe, *The House Church.* Nashville: Abingdon Press, 1975.

"Approaches to Intergenerational Education in the Church," Packet available from Educational Planning Services, American Baptist Churches in the U.S.A., Valley Forge, PA 19481, 1976.

Collins, Gary R., *Facing the Future: The Church and Family Together.* Waco, Tex.: Word Books, Publisher, 1976.

*Dalglish, William A., "The Family-Centered Model as an Option for the Church's Educational Work." Nashville: Division of Education, Board of Discipleship, The United Methodist Church, 1974.

Elkins, Dov Peretz, *Humanizing Jewish Life: Judaism and the Human Potential Movement.* New York: A. S. Barnes and Company, 1976.

Hendric, Lela, *Extended Family: Combining Ages in Church Experience.* Nashville: Broadman Press, 1979.

Henry, Mark and Mary Frances, *A Patchwork Family.* Nashville: Broadman Press, 1978.

Huck, Gabe, and Sloyan, Virginia, eds., *Parishes and Families: A Model for Christian Formation Through Liturgy.* Washington, D.C.: The Liturgical Conference, Inc., 1973.

Koehler, George E., *Learning Together: A Guide for Intergenerational Education in the Church.* Nashville: Division of Education, Board of Discipleship, The United Methodist Church, 1977.

Miller, Sherrod, *Marriages and Families: Enrichment Through Communication.* Beverly Hills, Calif.: Sage Publications, 1975.

Olsen, Charles M., *The Base Church: Creating Community Through Multiple Forms.* Atlanta, Ga.. Forum House, Publisher, 1973.

Otto, Herbert A., *The Family Cluster: A Multi-Base Alternative.* Beverly Hills, Calif.: Holistic Press, 1971.

Pearl, Virginia, C. S. J., *A Bunch of Daisies: Model for a Family Program.* Mission, Kans.: Sheed Andrews & McNeel, 1975.

Reisman, Bernard., *The Chavurah: A Contemporary Jewish Experience.* New York: Union of American Hebrew Congregations, 1977.

Rozeboom, John D., *Family Camping: Five Designs for Your Church.* Nashville: Local Church Education, Board of Discipleship, The United Methodist Church, 1973.

Sawin, Margaret M., "The Family Cluster: A Model for Religious Education," 1972. Available from Innovation Referral Service, Board of Discipleship, The United Methodist Church, Nashville, TN.

Sawin, Margaret M., "Adolescents Look at Family Cluster" in Huber, Evelyn, *Doing Christian Education in New Ways.* Valley Forge, Pa.: Judson Press, 1978.

*Sawin, Margaret M., "Educating by Family Groups: A New Model for Religious Education," 1977. A mimeographed monograph available from Family Clustering, Inc., P. O. Box 18074, Rochester, N.Y. 14618.

Sawin, Margaret M., "Community and Family: Growing Faith Through Family Clusters" in Harris, Maria, ed., *Parish Religious Education.* New York: Paulist Press, 1977.

*Smith, Leon, *Family Ministry: An Educational Resource for the Local Church.* Nashville: Division of Education, United Methodist Board of Discipleship, 1975.

United States Catholic Conference, Department of Education, *Family-Centered Catechesis: Guidelines and Resources.* Washington, D.C.: United States Catholic Conference, 1979.

VanderHaar, Delbert J., "Developing a Family Life Ministry in the Local Congregation" Orange City, Iowa: Reformed Church in America, 1975. (Mimeographed pamphlet available from Office of Family Life, Reformed Church in America, Orange City, IA 51041.)

Westerhoff, John H. III, and Neville, Gwen K. *Generation to Generation: Conversations on Religious Education and Culture.* Philadelphia: United Church Press, 1974.

D. For use with chapter 5—books which have exercises relating to thematic areas:

Agard, Bonnie, *Family Cluster Resources.* Chicago: Department of Christian Education, The Evangelical Covenant Church of America, 1977.

*Benson, Jeanette, S.P., and Hilyard, Jack L., *Becoming Family.* Winona, Minn.: St. Mary's College Press, 1979.

Brayer, Herbert O., and Cleary, Zella W., *Valuing in the Family: A Workshop Guide for Parents.* San Diego, Calif.: Pennant Press (a division of Progressive Playthings, Inc.), 1972.

Castle, David, *Toward Caring: People Building in the Family.* Richmond, Ind.: Friends United Press, 1973.

Coleman, Lyman, *Hassle: Dealing with Family Relationships.* Waco, Tex.: Creative Resources, 1975.

Doscher, Fred and Margaret Lee, *Mushroom Family.* A quarterly periodical with separate seasonal themes to use with families. Order from *Mushroom Family,* P. O. Box 12572, Pittsburgh, PA 15241.

Ecumenical Task Force on Christian Education for World Peace, *Try This: Family Adventures Toward Shalom.* Nashville: Discipleship Resources, United Methodist Church, 1979.

Glashagel, Jerry and Char, *Valuing Families: Tools for Values Education in Family Life.* New York: National Board of Young Men's Christian Associations, 1977.

Hartman, Larry, ed., *Love Happens in Families.* Chicago: Christian Family Movement, 1974.

Jeep, Elizabeth McMahon, and Huck, Gabe, *Celebrate Summer: A Guidebook for Families.* Paramus, N.J.: Paulist Press, 1973.

Larson, Roland S. and Doris E., *Values and Faith: Value-Clarifying Exercises for Family and Church Groups.* Minneapolis: Winston Press, 1976.

Lewis, Howard R., and Streitfeld, Harold S., *Growth Games: How to Tune in Yourself, Your Family, Your Friends.* New York: Bantam Books, 1972.

*Pfeiffer, J. William, and Jones, John E., *A Handbook of Structured Experiences for Human Relations Training,* vols. 1, 2, 3, 4, 5. San Diego: University Associates, Inc.. 1973-75.

Shadle, Carolyn, ed., "Bows and Arrows," a quarterly newsletter for family enrichment. Order from Interpersonal Communication Services, 7052 West Lane, Eden, New York 14057.

*Simon, Sidney B.; Howe, Leland W.; and Kirschenbaum, Howard, *Values Clarification: A Handbook of Practical Strategies for Teachers and Students.* New York: Hart Publishing Company, Inc., 1972.

E. **For use with Chapter 5—books which explicitly use biblical themes:**

Bock, Lois, and Working, Miji, *Happiness Is a Family Time Together.* Old Tappan, N.J.: Fleming H. Revell Company, 1975.

Breig, James, and Knopp, Patricia, S.N.D., *A Guide for Family Bible Reading.* Chicago: Claretian Publications, 1977.

Griggs, Donald and Patricia, *Generations Learning Together.* Livermore, Calif.: Griggs Educational Service, 1976.

May, Edward C., *Family Worship Idea Book.* St. Louis: Concordia Publishing House, 1965.

Nutting, R. Ted, *Family Cluster Programs: Resources for Intergenerational Bible Study.* Valley Forge, Pa.: Judson Press, 1977. (Although this book uses the title "Family Cluster Programs," it basically is utilizing another model of family enrichment than clusters.)

Rogers, Sharee and Jack, *The Family Together: Inter-generational Education in the Church School.* Los Angeles: Acton House, Inc., Publishers, 1976.

VanderHaar, Delbert and Trudy, "Celebrating Family Life," "Celebrating Thanksgiving," "Generations Learning Together in the Congregation," "Celebrating Peace—Love—Joy." Orange City, Iowa: Reformed Church in America, 1976. Mimeographed pamphlets available from Office of Family Life, Reformed Church in America, Orange City, IA 51041.

Wiencke, Gustav K., *A Summer Family Style Church School.* Philadelphia: Fortress Press, 1975.

Yearly Family Programs on different biblical, seasonal themes available from Religious Education Department, Glenmary Home Missioners, 2501 Ashwood Ave., Nashville, TN 37212.

Young, Lois Horton, *Dimensions for Happening: A New Method for Responding to the Bible Through Art.* Valley Forge, Pa.: Judson Press, 1971.

F. For use with chapters 5 and 6—books which interpret leadership skills and background knowledge for leaders:

Clinebell, Howard J., Jr., *The People Dynamic: Changing Self and Society Through Growth Groups.* New York: Harper and Row, Publishers, 1972.

Guerney, Bernard G., Jr., ed., *Psychotherapeutic Agents: New Roles for Non-Professionals, Parents and Teachers.* New York: Holt, Rinehart and Winston, Inc., 1969.

*Johnson, David W., *Reaching Out: Interpersonal Effectiveness and Self-Actualization.* Englewood Cliffs, N.J.: Prentice-Hall, Inc., 1972.

*Johnson, David W. and Frank P., *Joining Together: Group Theory and Group Skills.* Englewood Cliffs, N.J.: Prentice-Hall, Inc., 1975.

Kaplan, Ralph, *Little Objectives for Little People.* Campbell, Calif.: PBS, 1970 (A Product of Behavioral Sciences, Inc.). Order from PBS, 1140 Dell Ave., Campbell, CA 95008.

Mager, Robert F., *Preparing Instructional Objectives.* Palo Alto, Calif.: Fearon Publishers, 1962.

Monroe, Richard E., *Exploring Leadership Styles.* Nashville: Division of Education, Board of Discipleship, The United Methodist Church, 1972.

Schutz, William C., *Joy: Expanding Human Awareness.* New York: Grove Press, 1967.

Index